AN INTRODUCTION TO NANOCATALYST FOR ORGANIC SYNTHESIS

SYNTHESIS, CHARACTERIZATION AND CATALYTIC APPLICATIONS

DR. JITHENDRA KUMARA K S | PRASHANTHA M V | HARISH M C

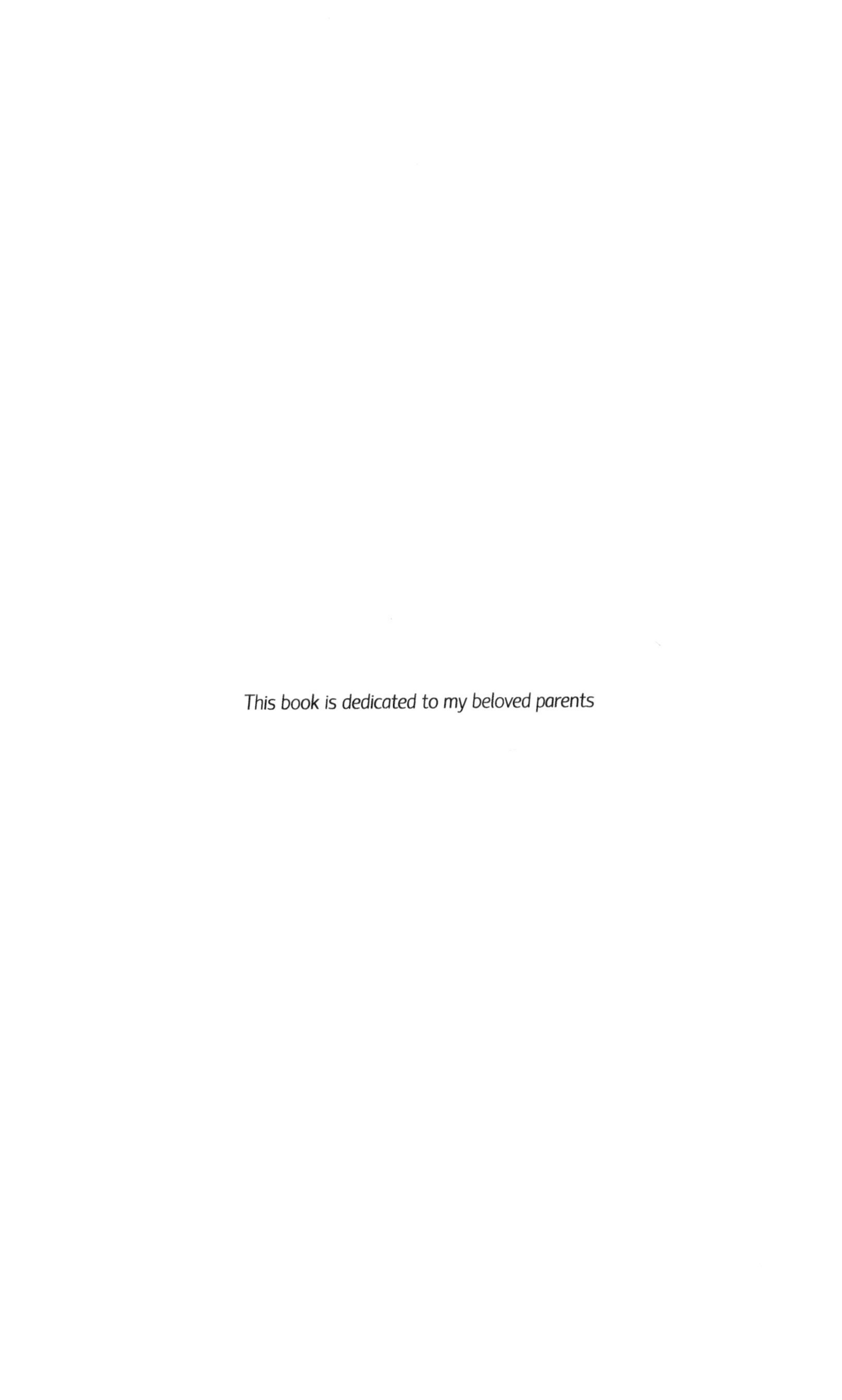

This book is dedicated to my beloved parents

Contents

Foreword

Dr. Ranjith Y

The publication with the title An Introduction to Nanocatalyst for Organic Synthesis has a lot of information that you can study it. You can get a lot of benefits after reading this book. This specific book exist new know-how the information that exists in this book represented the condition of the world right now. That is important to you to learn how the improvement the world. This particular book will bring you a new era of internationalization. You can read the e-book on your smartphone, so you can read that anywhere you want.

Dr. Usha jinendra

You will get this Basic concept of Nano Chemistry and its catalytic activity by visiting the bookstore or Mall. Just simply viewing or reviewing it could be your solution issue if you get difficulties with one's knowledge. Kinds of this reserve are various. Not only by simply written or printed and also can you enjoy this book by means of the e-book. In the modern era like now, you just look at your mobile phone and search what their problem is. Right now, choose your current ways to get more information about your book. It is most important to arrange yourself to make your knowledge still change. Let's try to choose the proper ways for you.

Preface

The development of green, sustainable, and economical chemical processes is one of the major challenges in chemistry. Besides the traditional need for efficient and selective catalytic reactions that will transform raw materials into valuable chemicals, pharmaceuticals, and fuels, green chemistry also strives for waste reduction, atomic efficiency, and high rates of catalyst recovery. Nanostructured materials are attractive candidates as heterogeneous catalysts for various organic transformations, especially because they meet the goals of green chemistry. Among these are novel approaches that have permitted the rational design and synthesis of highly active and selective nanostructured catalysts by controlling the structure and composition of the active nanoparticles (NPs) and by manipulating the interaction between the catalytically active NP species and their support. The ease of isolation and separation of the heterogeneous catalysts from the desired organic product and the recovery and reuse of these NPs further enhance their attractiveness as green and sustainable catalysts.

Although the past decade has brought many advances, there are still challenges in the area of nanocatalysis that need to be addressed. These include loss of catalytic activity during operation due to sintering, leaching of soluble species from the nanocatalysts under harsh reaction conditions, loss of control over well-defined morphologies during the scale-up synthesis of thc nanocomposites, and limited examples of enantioselective nanocatalytic systems. The future of nanocatalyst research lies in the judicious design and development of nanocomposite catalysts that are stable and resistant to sintering and leaching, and yet are highly active and enantioselective for the desired catalytic organic transformations, even after multiple runs. Nanotechnology will modify the environment both in a positive and negative way. On the one hand, new nanomaterials are promising for reducing greenhouse gases, cleaning toxic wastes and building alternative energy sources.

Dr. Jithendra Kumara K S
Prashantha M V
Harish M C

Acknowledgements

- I am Thankful to my Research guide and Chairman, Department of chemistry, Sahyadri Science College, Kuvempu University, Shivamogga.
- I profusely thankful to my beloved parents
- My sincere thanks to my colleagues in the department and students.

Prologue

This book covers the basics of nanotechnology and provides a solid understanding of the subject. Starting from a brush-up of basic nanochemistry and materials science, the book helps to gradually build up an understanding of the various fundamental concepts of nanochemistry and nanotechnology. The book covers the various physical, chemical, and hybrid methods of nanomaterial synthesis and nanofabrication as well as synthetic applications. It includes chapters on the various applications of nanoscience and nanotechnology. It is written in a simple form, making it useful for students of nanochemistry and material sciences.

Dr. Jithendra Kumara K S

Prashantha M V

Harish M C

CHAPTER ONE

Nanocatalyst

1. General Overview

Nanotechnology represents one of the key breakthroughs of present chemical science, enabling materials of unique size, structure, and composition to be formed. These nano-dimensional materials (in the 1–100 nm size domains) are serving as a bridge between atomic and bulk materials and have been to reveal a variety of novel chemical, physical and electronic properties [1]. The study of these nanoscale properties has become an increasingly important area in chemistry, physics, biology, medicine, and material sciences. However, trustworthy preparations of the nanomaterials are required for their utilization, and this area remains dynamic research. Moreover, many research has engaged on nanomaterials of the coinage metals (especially those of gold) [2], In addition to this, the studies of other transition metal properties are also considerable and growing [3]. The nanomaterial provides a high surface-area-to-volume ratio making nanomaterials highly desirable for use as a potential catalyst.

The synthesis of nanomaterial with the tuning of size and shape is a highly challenging task in nanochemistry [4-14]. The well-defined shape and narrow size distribution are very important for exhibiting potential practical applications. One particular purpose for undertaking such a synthesis is to study surface plasmon resonance, which is a feature dependent on the size and shape of the nanomaterials [11-17]. Examples of metal nanoparticles with size-dependent surface plasmon resonance are of CdSe, Pd, Ag, and Au [18-21]. Initially, researchers emphasized gold nanomaterial because when the anisotropic effect is added to Au nanoparticles it shows shape-dependent surface Plasmon resonance [22-24]. The fruitful synthesis of mono-dispersed metal nanoparticles also allows for the study of size-dependent on other properties such as catalytic activities and biological activities [25, 26]. A similar nanomaterial exhibits a higher catalytic activity because nanomaterial has a larger surface area and higher density of active sites, consequently, monodispersed nanomaterials are an essential subject and a prerequisite for functional purposes.

2. Nanochemistry and Nanomaterials

Nanomaterials generally refer to the nanometre scale, typically in the range of 1-100 nm, which exhibit outstanding properties compared to their bulk counterparts and are verified novel applications in various fields [27]. By the reason of this nanotechnology is closely related to all science disciplines, particularly in the field of chemistry (Figure 1.1). In nanochemistry, chemists successfully use a chemical approach and many tools of synthetic chemistry to construct individual atoms or molecules into nanomaterials in size and shape-controlled manner [28-31]. The surface properties of nanomaterials can be modified with the knowledge of coordination chemistry and fit for applications in various fields. Not only that the nanomaterial provides a high density of active surface area which is particularly used to modify organic transformation and organic synthesis with respect to the chemical and physical aspects of the reaction [32-35].

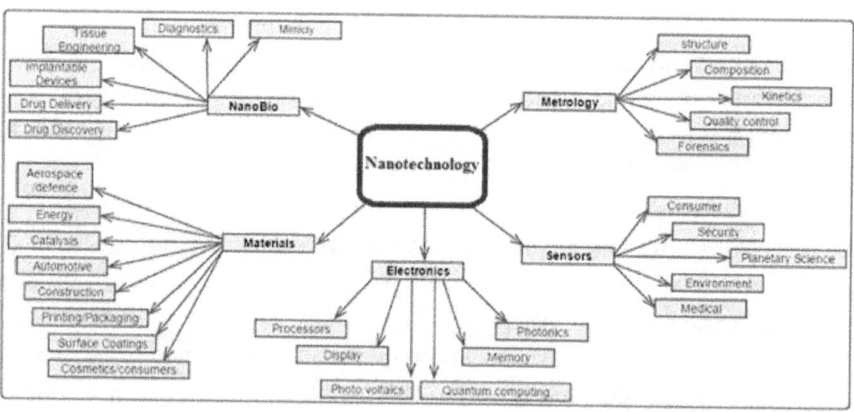

Fig.1.1. Nanotechnology is closely related to all aspects of science

The nanomaterials with different shapes can be synthesized. Numerous articles have been published dealing with the shape-controlled synthesis of nanocrystals [11-14]. Usually, nanomaterials morphology can be classified into three main categories: zero dimension (0D), one dimension (1D), and two dimensions (2D) nanomaterials [36-41]. Examples of the well-known morphologies are nanoparticles, nanowires, nanotubes, and nanoplates as depicted in Figure 1.2. All of these nanomaterials should have at least one dimension on the nanometer scale (1-100 nm).

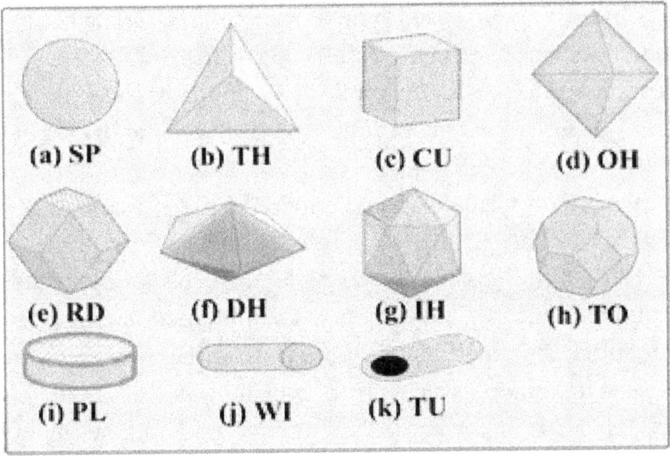

Fig.1.2. Schematic illustration of nanomaterials with various morphologies (a) sphere (SP), (b) tetrahedron (TH), (c) cube (CU), (d) octahedron (OH), (e) rhombic dodecahedron (RD) octahedron (OH), (f) decahedron (DH), (g) icosahedrons (IH), (h) truncated octahedron (TO) (i) plate (PL), (j) wire (WI), (k) tube (TU).

The synthetic path of the nanomaterials can mainly be divided into two approaches one is "top-down" and another one is "bottom-up" approaches (Figure 1.3). The "top-down" approach mainly gives attention to the reduction of the bulk systems into nanomaterials by using an external physical tool (s) such as a laser or photon beam or electron beam in chemical patterning and lithography technique [42]. However, the disadvantage of this approach is a large amount of material wasted during the process [43], which is objectionable in the context of green chemistry. In the "bottom-up" approach, meanwhile, the chemical reaction is used to assemble the smaller unit into larger nanomaterial [44-46].

However the prepared nanomaterial size and shape can be controlled down to several nanometers (<5 nm), because of the initial using "tiny" building units (molecules or atoms). The "bottom-up" approach allows controlling the growth rate at different crystal faces giving nanomaterials of assorted structures. As a result, the "bottom-up" approach is more advantageous and adopted by chemists in nanomaterials synthesis [44-46].

The synthetic protocol for the bottom-up approach can be classified mainly into gas-phase (or vapour-based) and liquid-phase (or solution-based) synthesis. Vapour-based synthesis of nanomaterials mainly involves the vapour-liquid-solid growth (VLS) and chemical vapour deposition (CVD) techniques [47, 48]. Examples of vapour-based synthesis are Ge nanowires [49-51], ZnO nanorods [41], Bi_2S_3 nanowires [52], CoS nanowires [53], and MnS nanowires [53]. Recently, Li and co-workers reported the general synthetic root of metal sulfide has a one-dimensional nanostructure by atmospheric pressure chemical vapour deposition (APCVD) [54]. These gas-phase synthetic protocols always require special handling and complicated instruments. The obtained nanocrystals are also in low quantity and productivity [54, 55]. However, solution-based synthesis of nanomaterials is more opportune, and easier to handle and no special apparatus is required. Moreover, the as-obtained nanomaterials can be directly employed in physiological study or later supported onto solid supports for catalysis. Huge efforts have been made by chemists to develop a solution-based synthesis of nanomaterials [45, 46, 56-59]. Thus, the synthesis of nanoparticles by the solution-based synthetic protocol is one of the main focuses of this thesis. Examples of solution-based synthetic strategies of nanomaterials that are used in our work are discussed below.

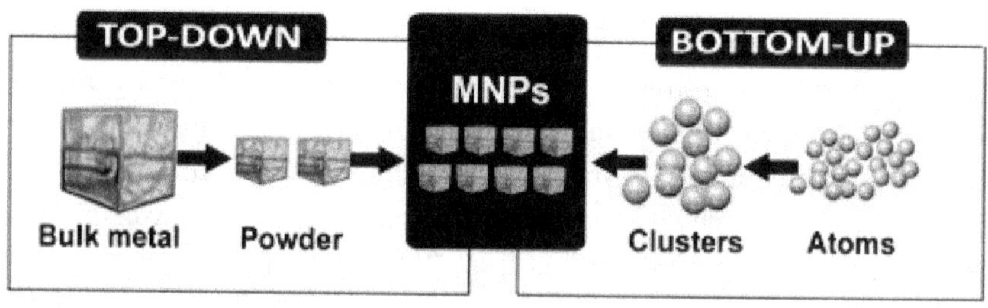

Fig.1.3. schematic illustration of top-down and bottom-up approaches towards the synthesis of nanomaterials

3. Synthesis of Ligand stabilized metal nanoparticles

It is well known that the physicochemical property of metal nanoparticles (or material) depends on their composition as well as structural parameters such as crystallite size, shape, and overall architecture [60]. Many strategies for achieving a high degree of controlled composition and size of metal nanomaterials are continually emerging. Recent examples include many routes to achieve shape-controlled nanocrystals [60, 61], symmetrically branched nanocrystals, [62–65] hierarchical/multimetal nanodendrites [66–69], and core-shell nanostructures, [70–72] to name a few. The overall quality of the nanomaterials with respect to their applications is controlled by the judicious selection of reagents such as metal precursors, solvents, capping agents, reducing agents, and other additives. However, once starting reagents are selected and incorporated into a synthesis, exchange processes and even reactions can occur between various components. Thus, the initial components may not contribute to the final product formation, and unexpected products can arise. For example, Soulantica and co-workers found in the synthesis of cobalt nanoparticles the amount of Co precursor added to the ligand solution resulted in an unanticipated side reaction (unrelated to the primary reaction responsible for product formation) that eventually defined the characteristics of the final Co nanocrystals [73]. Regrettably, the characterization of intermediates in nanomaterial syntheses is often overlooked but is a required step toward understanding the transformation taken from metal precursor to metal nanostructure.

The environment of ligands in metal complexes determines their overall thermodynamic and kinetic stability. Some well-known examples comprise the design of bulky ligands to avoid metal-catalyzed oligomerization reactions that are otherwise thermodynamically favored as well as polydentate ligands that provide thermodynamic stabilization via the chelate or macrocyclic effect [74]. The principles outlined in coordination chemistry provide an extensive library of potential complexes to consider as precursors to metal nanostructures. In practice, common metal halide salts or commercially available organometallic complexes are often used; the local ligand environment in metal precursors is created through the addition of extraneous reagents. For example, introduced capping agents (molecules or ions that adsorb to metal nanoparticle surfaces to provide stabilization) can be exchanged with the native ligands of metal precursors in a system if their binding affinity for the metal center of the precursor is greater than that of the native ligands [75,76]. When such exchange processes occur, in addition to their primary role of particle stabilization, the capping agents take on a secondary role by manipulating the kinetic and thermodynamic stability of the metal precursor. The possible roles of ligands in nanomaterials syntheses include but are not limited to (i) coordination with metal centers to determine the kinetic and thermodynamic stability of precursors, (ii) coordination with the surfaces of nanoparticles to provide colloidal stability, (iii) coordination to the surfaces of nanoparticles to provide structure direction, (iv) a source of reducing agent, and (v) an oxidative etchant.

The ligand will play a dual role in nanoparticle synthesis first, as capping agents are employed in nanomaterial syntheses to provide colloidal stability and direct the growth of nanocrystals into required forms. These capping agents may come directly from the ligand sphere of metal precursors or can also be incorporated into a synthesis. In the latter case, the extraneous capping agents are surface ligands that may also displace the native ligands of a metal complex and modify the kinetics of the precursor.

The review of the literature shows that the sulfur-containing ligands show highly efficient stabilizers for nanoparticles. It also reveals, the strong interaction between platinum group metal and soft sulfur-based lingad for example, in the 1990s, Brust and co-workers demonstrated that the thiols group made excellent stabilizers in the two-phase preparation of gold nanoparticles (77). The use of sulfur-based ligands to stabilize palladium nanoparticles usually restricts their use as potential catalysts due to the poisoning effect of sulfur (78). However, this effect is not universal. For example, dodecylthiolate **1** (**Figure 1.4**) stabilized palladium nanoparticles have been shown to be active catalysts for the formation of carbon nanotubes (79). Furthermore, they have been demonstrated to be a stable and recyclable catalyst in the Suzuki-Miyaura C–C coupling reaction of haloarenes and phenylboronic acid (80), while the palladium nanoparticles stabilized by thiolated-β-cyclodextrin (HS-β-CD) **2** (**Figure 1.4**) show good activity in the hydrogenation of allylamine (81, 82). The two-phase Brust methodology can also be used to protect palladium nanoparticles by using alkanethiol like S-dodecylthisulfate ligand **3** (**Figure 1.4**).

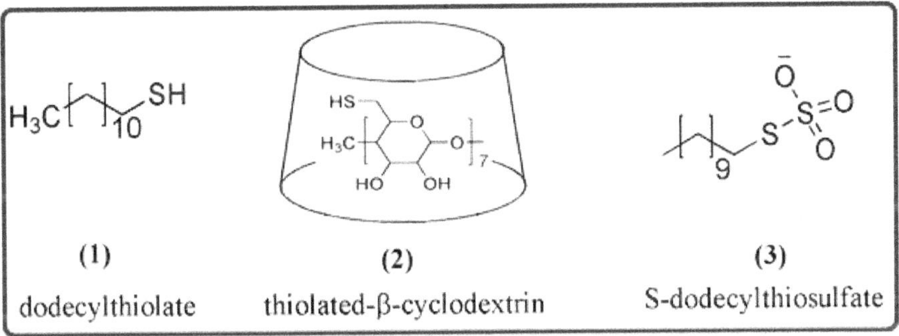

Fig.1.4. reported thiol ligands for stabilization of palladium nanoparticles

The presence of the chelating diphosphine ligands provided remarkable stability to the nanoparticles, the preparation of palladium nanoparticles by using a phosphine-stabilizer has also been undertaken by Fujihara et al. using a two-phase process. They adapted an existing route for preparing related to gold nanoparticles (83) by phase transferring potassium tetrachloropalladate(II) as a precursor in the presence of optically active bidentate BINAP (2,2-bis(diphenylphosphino)-1,1'-binaphthyl) ligands **4** (**Figure 1.5**). The use of chiral (*R*)- and (*S*)-BINAP **5** (**Figure 1.5**) gave rise to the corresponding chiral palladium nanoparticles, hence circular dichroism spectra showed positive and negative Cotton effects, respectively,

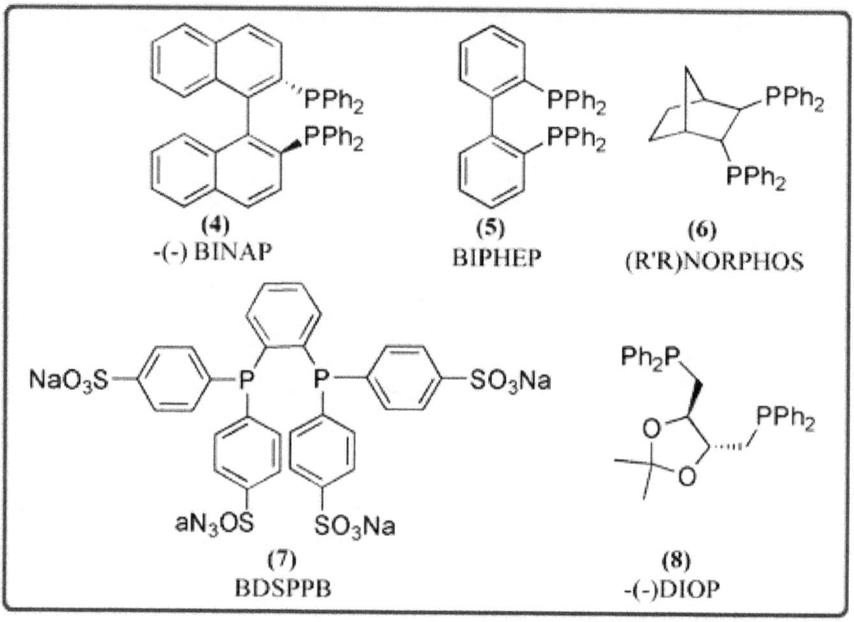

Fig.1.5. Reported phosphine ligands for stabilization of palladium nanoparticles [84]

The electron-rich nitrogen-donating ligands have been extensively used to stabilize precious metal nanoparticles. The lone pair of the nitrogen species (such as long-chain primary amines) is able to strongly chemically adsorb onto the surface of the metal, with the alkyl group preventing agglomeration *via* steric stabilization. In another reported method, mono dispersed palladium nanoparticles are synthesized by using oleylamine **9** (**Figure 1.5**) which is served as a solvent stabilizing ligand and reductant, along with tributylamine (BTB) **10** (**Figure 1.5**) as a co-reductant. In addition to aliphatic amines, numerous other nitrogen-containing molecules have been used to stabilize palladium nanoparticles. These include aromatic amines **11** (**Figure 1.5**) (85), porphyrins **12** (86), and imidazole derivatives **13** (87) pyridyl groups **14** (88). Recently, Serpell *et al.* have prepared a highly active palladium nanocatalyst for hydrogenation reaction in which imidazole derivatives are used as effective stabilizers and subsequently deposited onto the active carbon (87).

As far as noble metals are concerned, some important bulky ligands are used to stabilize the palladium metal nanoparticles and control their growth. J. Huang, et al. [89] report the hydrogenation of olefins in [BMIM][PF$_6$] catalyzed by phenanthroline (Phen) **15** (**Figure 1.7**) ligand-protected palladium nanoparticles. Recently, Sekar et al. reported the efficiency and reusability of palladium nanoparticles stabilized by Pd–binaphthyl **16** (**Figure 1.7**) ligand in the Heck, Suzuki–Miyaura, and Sonogashira cross-coupling reactions [90]. In Gopidas's work [91], for an instance, the palladium nanoparticles stabilized by Pd–G1-dendrimer carbon bonds were synthesized and applied to the reduction of carbon-carbon multiple bonds. T. Mayer-Gall et al. [92] demonstrated the influence of pyridyl-substituted porphyrins stabilized palladium nanoparticles with respect to the competing coordination sites: central pyrrole nitrogens versus peripheric pyridyl nitrogens.

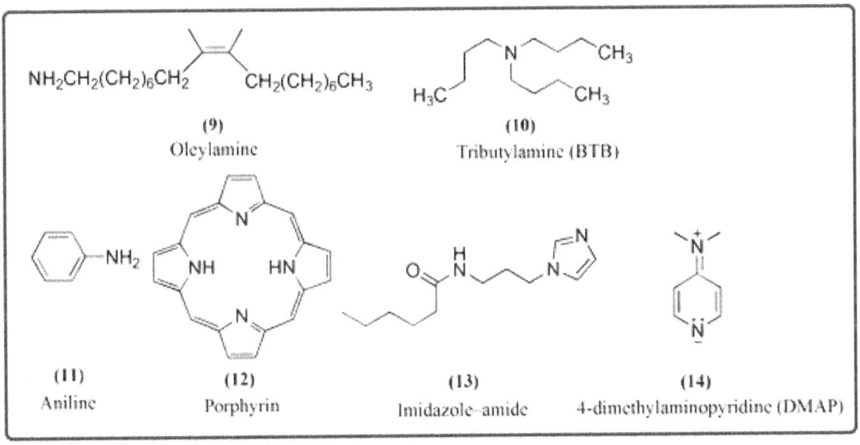

Fig.1.6. reported amine stabilized nitrogen-containing ligands for stabilization of nanoparticles

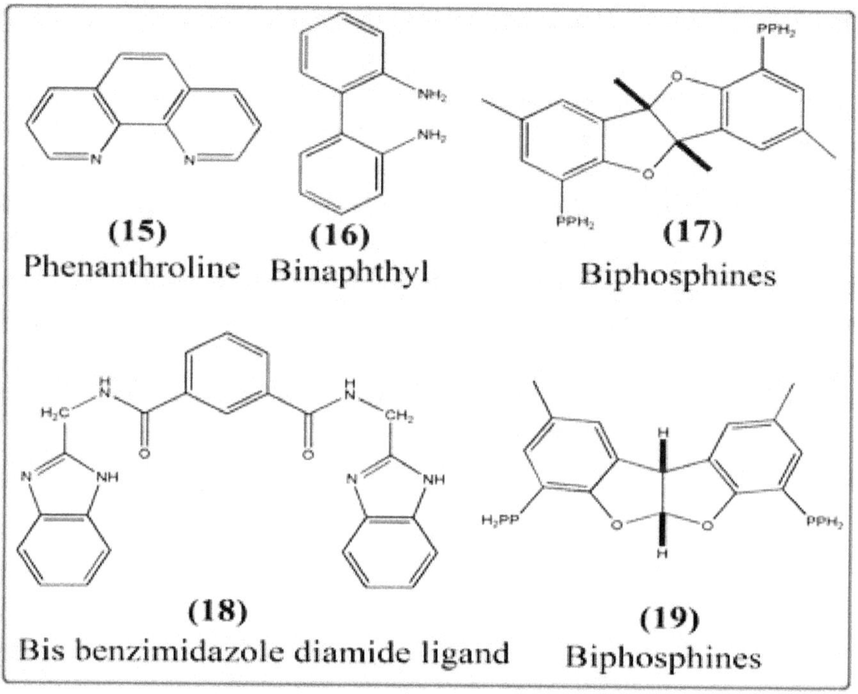

Fig.1.7. Some important bulky ligands are used to stabilize the palladium metal nanoparticles

Along with this M. Singla et al. [93] showed that metal salts are being capped by a bis benzimidazole diamide **18 (Figure 1.7)** organic moiety forming stable nano coordination compounds or nanocomposites for size and co-anion dependent study of conductivity, and the correlation of band gap studies with conductivity, in addition to this Galvez et al. [94] reported that roof-shaped diphosphines and monophosphine **17, 19 (Figure 1.7)** were used for making nanometal composite that was used in catalytic activity.

4. Synthesis of metal nanoparticles by seed-mediated growth method

The formation of metal nanoparticles in solution-phase consists of a long chain of reaction steps. Generally, these steps could be divided into two different stages: nucleation and growth. During the nucleation stage, the reduction or decomposition of metal precursors leads to the formation of metal atoms. These metal atoms then self-assemble into small clusters and further grow into relatively stable crystal nuclei. In the growth stage, these crystal nuclei serve as seeds for the subsequent growth of metal nanoparticles. Based on the temporal and spatial differences between the nucleation and growth stages, the synthesis of metal nanoparticles can be divided into two major categories: homogeneous nucleation and heterogeneous nucleation [95]. For homogeneous nucleation, the seed nanoparticles are generated in situ. The nucleation and growth of metal nanoparticles are normally realized through the same chemical reaction. For the heterogeneous nucleation, the seed nanoparticles are pre-synthesized and added into a growth solution to further grow into metal nanoparticles.

A typical seed-mediated growth process involves the preparation of metal seed nanoparticles and their subsequent growth in reaction solutions containing metal precursors, reducing reagents, and shape-directing reagents [96]. The most commonly used shape-directing reagents are cationic surfactants, such as cetyltrimethylammonium bromide (CTAB) **20** (**Figure 1.8**), cetylpyridinium chloride (CPC) **21** (**Figure 1.8**) and Benzyldimethylammoniumchloride (BDAC) **22** (**Figure 1.8**) [97]. In the growth stage, the reduction of metal precursors preferentially occurs on the surface of the seeds due to their catalytic properties, leading to the further growth of metal-metal nanoparticles. Compared with other methods, the nucleation and growth stages of the seed-mediated growth of metal nanoparticles are well separated, and thus better control over the size, size distribution, and shape evolution of metal-metal nanoparticles is provided. Because of these advantages, the seed-mediated growth method is especially promising in providing mechanistic insights into the growth mechanisms of metal-metal nanoparticles.

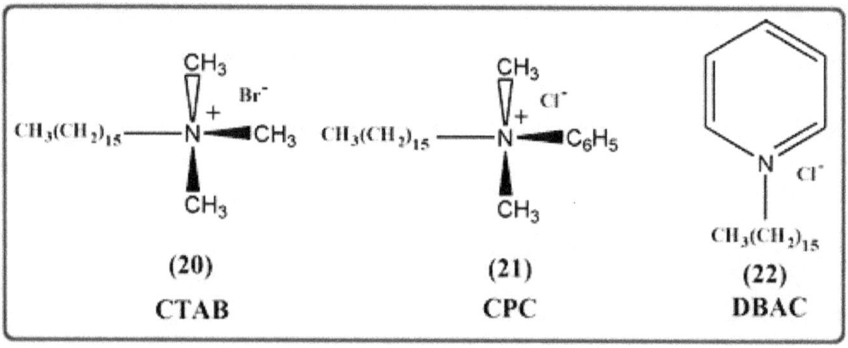

Fig.1.8. commonly used shape-directing reagents are cationic surfactants

The seed-mediated growth method is well known for its effectiveness in the size control of metal nanoparticles [96, 98]. For example, Jana and coworkers prepared 20-100 nm spherical gold nanoparticles in diameter with narrow size distributions by using the seed-mediated growth method [99]. On the Bases of the "large seed" strategy, we can simultaneously control the crystal structures and the sizes of metal nanocrystals. For example, monodisperse Pd nano Cu- bes with different sizes were synthesized through the seed-mediated growth method [10]. The final edge length of nanocubes could be easily tuned by adding different volumes of seed solution. This method is able to produce monodisperse Pd nanocubes in high yields with broad size control from 22 to 109 nm. Brown and Natan reported a growth route to synthesize Au nanoparticles spanning from 30 to 100 nm based on 12 nm seeds via surface-catalyzed reduction of Au^{3+} with hydroxylamine. [100] Jana et al. reported a seed-based synthesis of Au nanoparticles via the gradual addition of ascorbic acid during the growth stage.[101,102] Pal and co-workers have reported a seed-mediated growth method for the synthesis of Au nanoparticles using photochemically prepared seed particles.[103,104] Cubic copper nanoparticles were also synthesized following a similar seed-mediated process from the same group.[105] Feng Ye et al. demonstrated the synthesis of ruthenium nanoparticles in oleylamine, including the tuning of their morphology/ shape by temperature or by seed-mediated growth.

Seed-mediated growth has been well-documented as a most powerful route to synthesizing bimetallic core-shell nanoparticles [106, 107]. In a typical seed-mediated growth method, pre-formed seeds of one metal serve as nucleation sites for further growth of another metal. During subsequent reductive growth of the metal shell, sophisticated and careful control is required to avoid individual nucleation and growth of the secondary metal as individual particles. Liyu Chen et al [108] reported that a simple, efficient approach for the preparation of ultrafine Pd@Ag core-shell NPs within the pores of metal-organic framework (MOF) under a seed-mediated growth strategy with activated hydrogen atoms as reducing agent. Seed-mediated growth was also used to synthesize some asymmetric inorganic hybrid nanomaterials, Arnaud Mayence et al [109]. demonstrated that the synthesis of asymmetric iron-manganese (Fe-Mn) oxides hybrid nanoparticles using iron oxides nanocubes as seeds for the subsequent growth of manganese oxide, recently cobalt hexacyanoferrate nanoparticles (CoNPs) are used in fabrication work through seed-mediated method [110] R. Sivakumar et al. [111] describes a simple, inexpensive, seed-mediated and catalyst-free two-step aqueous solution growth approach for the preparation of different ZnO nanostructures.

5. magnetically separable cobalt ferrite (Co@Fe$_2$O$_4$) and ruthenium ferrite (Ru@Fe$_2$O$_4$) nanoparticles

a) Cobalt ferrite (Co@Fe$_2$O$_4$) nanoparticles

Magnetic nanoparticles which exhibit a variety of unique magnetic phenomena that are drastically different from those of their bulk counterparts, attain significant interest since these properties can be advantageous for utilization in a variety of applications (112) including magnetic fluids, catalysis, bio-applications, magnetic resonance imaging, and data storage. (113).

The magnetic properties of nanoparticles are determined by many factors, the key of these including the chemical composition, the type of the crystal lattice, the particle size and shape, the morphology, the interaction of the particle with the surrounding matrix and the neighboring particles. By changing the size, shape, composition, and structure of nanoparticles, the magnetic properties of the materials can be controlled (114).

Cobalt ferrite nanoparticles have a high coercivity and moderate saturation magnetization [115]. Cobalt ferrite nanoparticles have been widely used in many applications due to their high electromagnetic properties, good chemical stability, and mechanical hardness. Due to these properties, cobalt ferrites are used in video and audio tapes, high-density digital recording media in spintronics, solar cells, sensors, and catalysis [116]. Cobalt ferrites are used for applications in magnetic resonance imaging (MRI), magnetic fluid hyperthermia (MFH), biosensors, ferrofluids, magnetic separations, storage of magnetic materials, and targeted and controlled drug delivery [117, 118].

The saturation magnetization (Ms) of cobalt ferrite nanoparticles is smaller than that of the bulk and Ms decreases with a decrease in size. When the crystallite size is approximately equal to the single domain size then the coercivity reaches its maximum value. Cobalt ferrite nanoparticles have an inverse spinel structure. In this O^{2-} form FCC close packing, and Co^{2+} and Fe^{3+} occupy either tetrahedral or octahedral interstitial sites. In this inverse spinel cobalt ferrite structure, half of the Fe^{3+} ion and Co^{2+} ions occupy the octahedral sites, and the rest of the Fe^{3+} ions occupy the tetrahedral sites.

Kim et al. reported thatthesynthesized magnetic cobalt ferrite nanoparticles by temperature controlled co-precipitation method. It was observed that size and magnetic behavior depend on pH, salt concentration, temperature, and stirring speed of the solution. The physical size was laying between 2-15 nm both particle size and saturation magnetization (Ms) increases with an increase in synthesis temperature [119]. Hedayati et al. demonstrated that synthesized cobalt ferrite nanoparticles by chemical precipitation method, the sample exhibit superparamagnetism. The saturation magnetization (Ms) of the sample was 5.4 emu/g and coercivity was very small even less than 5 Oe. After heating, it showed ferromagnetism with Ms 32 emu/g and coercivity 150 Oe [120]. Huixia et al. prepared cobalt ferrite nanoparticles by reverse coprecipitation method. Particles were prepared at different pH and aging temperatures. It was concluded that the particle size increased with aging temperature and saturation magnetization did not exhibit a particular trend [121]. Jianmin Chen et al. reported that the synthesis of $Ag(0)/SiO_2$-$CoFe_2O_4$ NCs using Ammonia borane (NH_3BH_3) as a reductant via an impregnation-reduction route and their catalysis for hydrolytic dehydrogenation of Ammonia borane.[122] M. Kaya et al. investigated the magnetic, silica-coated cobalt(II) ferrite

SiO2/CoFe2O4 followed by in situ reductions of the Cu(II) ions on the surface of magnetic particles during the hydrolysis of Ammonia borane at room temperature [123]. R. S. Gaikwad et al. reported that Cobalt ferrite, $CoFe_2O_4$, and nanocrystalline films were deposited using the electrostatic spray method and explored in sustainable hydrogen production applications [124].

b) Ruthenium ferrite (Ru@Fe₂O₄) nanoparticles

Recently, the use of magnetic materials as catalyst support has attracted much attention, [125] because solid catalysts with magnetic properties can efficiently be separated from the reaction mixture by applying an external magnetic field. [126] This green and sustainable approach has many advantages since it is a fast, economical, and environmentally acceptable way of product separation and catalyst recycling. [127]

Magnetic nanoparticles mainly of Fe_3O_4, γ-Fe_2O_3, or Co have been widely studied, especially for medical diagnostics, magnetic hyperthermia treatment, imaging, and data storage; [128] magnetically separable materials have also found catalytic applications. [129] While silica-coated Fe_3O_4 nanoparticles decorated with metallic palladium (nanoPd@Fe_3O_4) have been synthesized and reported to catalyze the hydrogenation of cyclohexene to cyclohexane, [130] for ruthenium only ruthenium complexes supported on Fe_3O_4 are known [Ru(binap$'$)(dpen)-Cl_2] bound to Fe_3O_4 (binap$'$ = (R)-2,2$'$-bis(diphenylphosphino)-1,1$'$-binaphthyl-4phosphonic acid, dpen = (R,R)-1,2diphenylethylenediamine) as a catalyst for the asymmetric hydrogenation of ketones [131] and [Ru(OH)x] supported on Fe_3O as a catalyst for the hydration of nitriles to amides.[132] So far, magnetically recoverable metallic ruthenium is only known to be supported by $NiFe_2O_4$ nanoparticles, which catalyze the hydrogenation of alkynes to alkanes. [133] Despite the interesting catalytic potential to be expected from such a material, Fe_3O_4 nanoparticles decorated with metallic ruthenium (nanoRu@Fe_3O_4) have never been reported to the best of our knowledge. The easy separability of magnetic nanoparticles from a reaction mixture by means of an external magnet makes nanoRu@Fe_3O_4 an interesting material for catalytic transformations.

6. Catalytic Mizoroki-Heck coupling reaction

Palladium-catalyzed carbon–carbon bond-forming reactions developed by Heck, Negishi, and Suzuki, among others (Scheme 1) have made a critical impact on synthetic organic chemistry. [134,135] In this regard, coupling reactions present wide applications in the production of polymers, agrochemicals, pharmaceutical intermediates, and high-tech materials. [135,137] This widespread use is mainly due to the mild conditions associated with these reactions together with their tolerance to a wide variety of functional groups. However, the significance of carbon–carbon coupling reactions for both academic and industrial research is far from settled down. The recent methods for the development of new catalysts [138,139] have broadened enormously the potential uses of these processes. Thus, Pd holds a particularly prominent place because its significance in synthesis is not limited to carbon-carbon bond formation, and is documented in several well-renowned treatises.

Over the last decade, the use of transition metal nanoparticles (NPs) in catalysis has expanded considerably and has led to interesting applications. Their use in C–C bond formation reactions constitutes one of their most important applications, including the Suzuki, Heck, Sonogashira, Stille, Hiyama3, and Negishi reactions (Scheme 1). Because sustainable development involves the utilization of reusable catalysts, the search for new catalytic systems to replace existing homogeneous ones is one important issue.

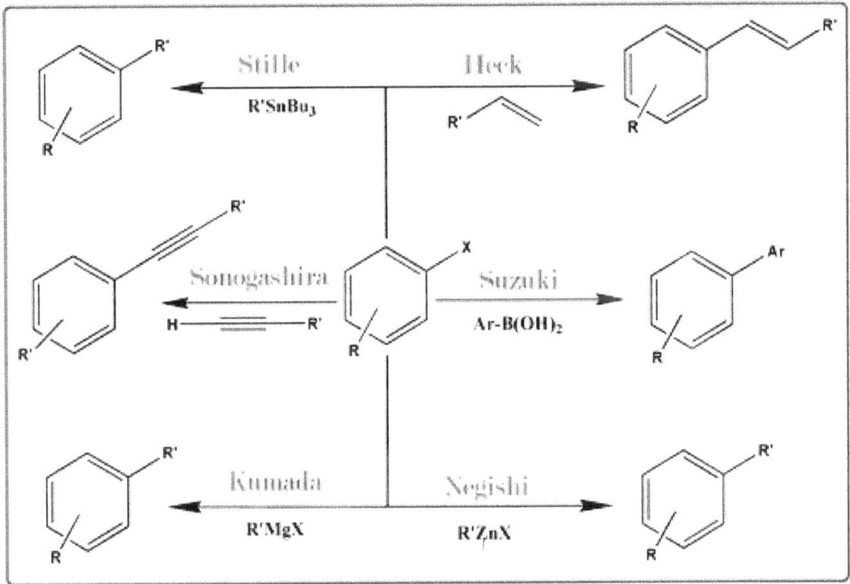

Scheme.1.1. Most Representative Pd-Catalyzed Carbon–Carbon Bond-Forming Cross-Coupling Reactions (where X = Cl, Br, or I)

The mechanisms of these reactions vary in many different aspects when examined in detail, but they share a number of common steps. Step 1) the formation of an R–Pd(II) intermediate from the starting organohalide and Pd(0)-catalyst, via an oxidative addition mechanism; [140] Step 2) transmetallation of an organic R2 substituent from the main group metal to the previously formed Pd(II) intermediate; [141] Step 3) Formation of a new carbon–carbon σ-bond between the R1 and R2 moieties through reductive elimination, which releases and regenerates Pd(0) that can partake in a new cycle. [142] While initiated by oxidative addition, the subsequent steps in the Mizoroki-Heck reaction

The Mechanism differs from the above-mentioned cross couplings (Scheme 3). Since olefins are used instead of organometallic substrates, the mechanism thus lacks a transmetallation step. Instead, in Step 2, the olefin will coordinate the Ar–Pd intermediate to form a π-complex. Step 3 comprises a carbopalladation, in which the aryl moiety in the Ar–Pd intermediate inserts into the double bond to form a σ–complex. This is followed by an internal rotation of the Cα–Cβ bond (with respect to Pd, not shown) and β–hydride elimination (Step 4). In Step 5, the newly formed Heck product is released from the Pd–hydride, which in turn is deprotonated by the base (Step 6) which regenerates the Pd(0)-catalyst. [143]

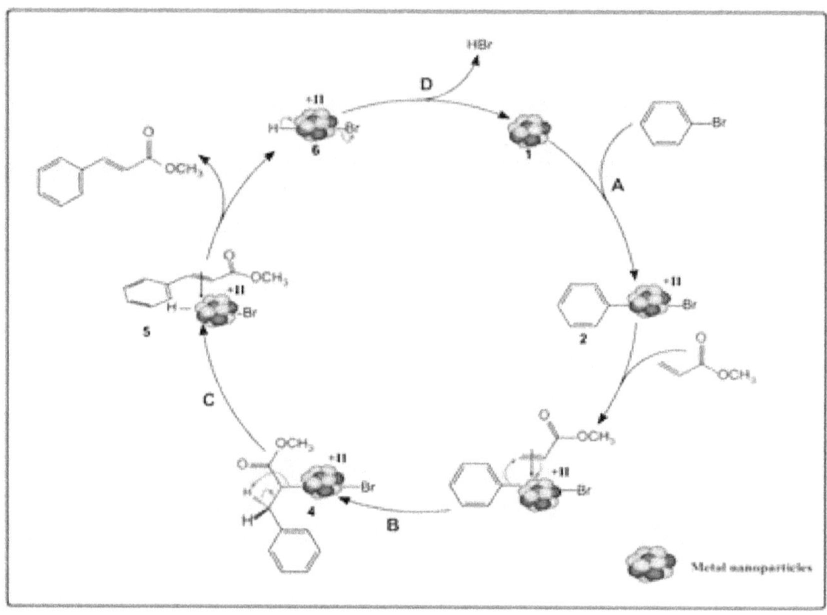

Scheme.1.2. General mechanism of cross-coupling reactions and the Heck–Mizoroki reaction

The first use of Pd NPs in the Heck reaction was reported by Beller et al. in 1996 using colloids stabilized by tetraoctylammonium bromide (TOA) prepared by reduction of [PdCl₂] in the presence of ammonium boronate. [144] These systems provided good results for the Heck arylation of styrene or butyl acrylate by activated aryl bromides at relatively low catalyst loading (0.05 mol%), but showed only limited activity for deactivated aryl bromides and aryl chlorides

Reetz and co-workers reported independently in 1996 the preparation of Pd NPs prepared by electrochemical reduction and stabilized by propylene carbonate. [145] Their size was 8–10 nm. This system successfully converted activated aryl bromides in high yields and also activated chlorobenzene with up to 30% conversion using 3.5 mol% Pd loadings.

Later, studying the Heck reaction of iodobenzene with ethyl acrylate in N-methyl pyrrolidinone (NMP), the same authors observed the formation of Pd nanoparticles of ca. 1.6 nm. Evidence that oxidative addition of iodobenzene occurs at the Pd NPs was obtained by addition of iodobenzene to preformed Pd NPs, which led to the formation of $[PhPdX3]^{2-}$ through leaching from the NP surface (Scheme 2). [146]

Numerous stabilizers and/or supports were used to form Pd NPs active in the Heck coupling reaction. The most common are based on polymeric and co-polymeric structures. Bradley and Blackmond reported a series of homopolymer-stabilized Pd NPs of distinct size and used them in the Heck reaction between 4-bromobenzaldehyde and butyl acrylate with a catalyst loading of 0.025 mol%. [147] Interestingly, the authors found that the initial rate increases with decreasing particle size, and a good correlation between the initial rate and the number of defect sites, concluding that the defect sites are the active centers in the Heck reaction. Trzeciak and co-workers reported the use of Pd nanoparticles stabilized by polyvinylpyrrolidone (PVP) as highly active catalysts for the Heck reaction of bromobenzene with butyl acrylate in $[Bu_4N]Br$ media.[148]

In 2004, Pd NPs stabilized by inorganic materials are reported, Shi and co-workers reported the use of a thin Pd NP layer on the pore channel surface of a mesoporous silica SBA-15, obtained through impregnation with a solution of $[Pd(OAc)_2]$ in THF followed by "in situ" reduction. [149] The material promoted the Heck reaction of aryl iodides and activated aryl bromides with styrene or methyl acrylate at 0.02 mol% catalyst loading, showing excellent recyclability similarly palladium nanoparticles were also stabilized by ionic liquid Dupont and co-workers described the behavior of Pd nanoparticles stabilized in imidazolium ionic liquids as catalyst (0.001 mol%) in the Heck reaction between butyl acrylate and aryl iodides.[150] The TEM images obtained before and after catalysis showed significant changes in Pd particle size. In addition, significant Pd leaching was observed and shown to vary during the course of the reaction. These results are coherent with the hypothesis that the Pd nanoparticles act as reservoirs of active species.

The immobilization of Pd nanoparticles on carbon nanostructures as supports for C–C coupling reactions has been applied extensively.[151] Gupton and co-workers reported the microwave-assisted synthesis of Pd NPs supported on graphene by the reduction of an aqueous mixture of Pd salt and dispersed graphite oxide sheets.[152] These NPs were shown to be highly active under microwave conditions, reaching significant turnover frequency values for aryl bromides. These catalysts were also able to convert 4-nitro-1-chlorobenzene and could be recycled several times without activity loss. Magnetic NPs have also been used as support materials for the adsorption of Pd NPs, which were reported as highly active catalysts in the Suzuki and Heck coupling reactions of aryl bromides.[153] These catalysts were efficiently recycled several times.

7. Catalytic Suzuki–Miyaura coupling reaction

The Suzuki cross-coupling has proven to be one of the most popular in the last years. Besides the mild reaction conditions associated with this method, one of the key assets of this preference is the availability of diverse boronic acids and the easy handling and removal of boron-containing byproducts when compared to other organometallic reagents. Thus, the effect of the size and shape of NPs on the catalytic activity of these reactions will be assessed. Likewise, the stability and recycling ability of Pd NPs together with the influence of different reaction parameters will also be brought up for consideration.

Suzuki-Miyaura reaction is characterized by a cross-coupling of two aryl sub-units, one from an aryl boronic acid or its derivative and the other from an organohalide or triflate to give a biaryl motif. [154-158] The relative reactivity order : R-I > R-OTf > R-Br >> RCl. This reaction becomes one of the most adaptable methods for the expansion of the carbon framework in organic molecules since its discovery in 1979. [159,160] Amongst its wide applicability; the Suzuki-Miyaura reaction is particularly useful as a way for the assembly of conjugated diene and higher polyene systems of high stereoisomeric purity as well as of biaryl and related systems. Incredible progress has been made in the development of Suzuki-Miyaura coupling reactions of unactivated alkyl halides, enabling C(sp2)–C(sp3) and even C(sp3)–C(sp3) bond-forming processes.[161-164] The non-toxicity and simplicity related to the preparation of organoboron compounds (e.g. aryl, vinyl, alkyl); [165,166] their relative stability to air and water, combined with the relatively mild conditions for the reaction as well as the formation of nontoxic by-products, makes Suzuki-Miyaura reaction an important method for enlarging carbon skeleton. The general and widely accepted mechanism of the Suzuki-Miyaura reaction is depicted in figure 1. The first step is the oxidative addition of palladium **1** to halide **2** to form the organopalladium species **3**. The reaction of organopalladium species with base gives intermediate **4**, which via transmetalation with the boron-ate complex **6** forms the organopalladium species **8**. Reductive elimination of the desired product **9** restores the original palladium catalyst **1**.

Recently two review articles have been published regarding this matter Balanta et al.[167] have outlined a general and objective description of PdNP-catalyzed carbon–carbon bond-forming processes, highlighting recent work in this area considering the stabilizing agents, catalytic results, and recycling possibilities. Likewise, Fihri et al. [168] have presented a broad overview of nanocatalysts for Suzuki cross-coupling reactions, emphasizing their performance, stability, and reusability.

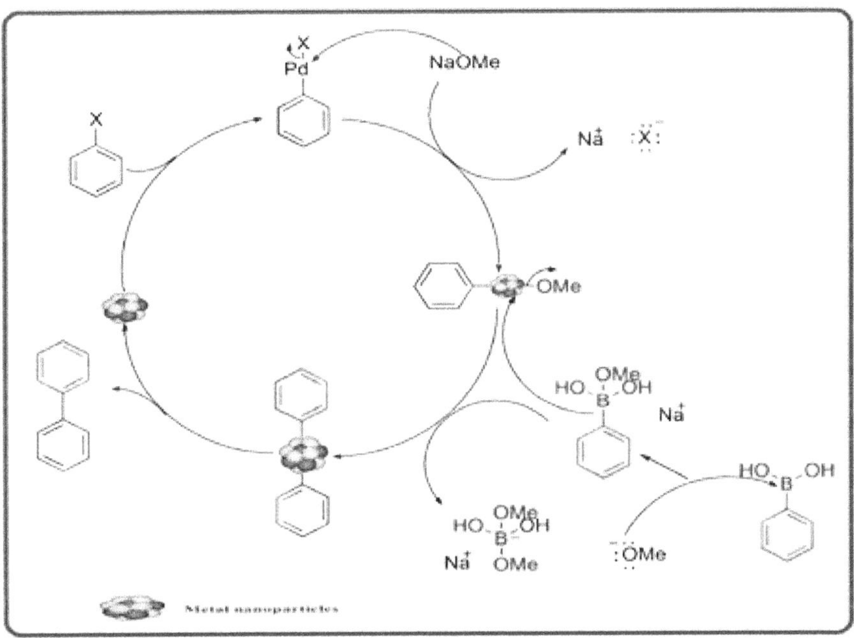

Scheme.1.3. General mechanism of cross-coupling reactions and the Suzuki cross coupling reaction

There are a variety of methods used for the production of transition-metal nanoparticles, and also a wide choice of solid supports, ranging from polymers to ordered mesoporous and modified silica. However, silica as solid support is a good choice because of its wide accessibility, excellent stability, porosity, and inert environment for the immobilization of transition-metal nanoparticles. [169-171] Pd nanoparticle catalysts have been introduced in mesoporous silica via several methods, such as ion exchange, wetness impregnation, chemical vapour infiltration, and in situ reductions. Gao and co-workers have reported a simple one-step method to synthesize palladium nanoparticles in highly ordered mesoporous channels of SBA-15 (Santa Barbara amorphous type silica), which has a pore size in the range of 5–10 nm, a large specific surface area, and a highly ordered pore structure. [172] The authors have indicated that the catalyst showed good activity for the Suzuki coupling of activated aryl bromides (80–99%) at 85 °C using K_2CO_3 as a base. However, the coupling of deactivated aryl bromides required longer times and gave lower yields than the activated aryl bromides. The catalysts were reused at least five cycles without a significant loss of efficiency.

In a recent study, Song and co-workers prepared an excellent non-reactor that was composed of hollow spheres of mesoporous silica with Pd nanoparticles residing inside the spheres [173]. This catalyst showed good activity in the coupling of aryl iodides with phenylboronic acids using K_2CO_3 as a base in refluxing ethanol. Pd leaching is substantially reduced in the composite, which enables stable catalytic performance. Unfortunately, recycling experiments were not reported for this system.

Like silica, metal oxides and double hydroxides can also be used to prepare nanocatalysts for Suzuki coupling reactions. For example, highly basic nanocrystalline magnesium oxide (MgO)-stabilized palladium NPS were prepared by counter ion stabilization of $PdCl_4^{2-}$ with nanocrystalline MgO followed by reduction. [174] This catalyst was found to be very active in the Suzuki cross-coupling of aryl bromides and iodides with several arylboronic acids in pure water at room temperature. Using 0.5 mol% of this catalyst in the presence of K_2CO_3 as a base, cross-couplings were completed in only 5 to 6 h at room temperature.

Like magnesium oxide, nanostructured zirconium oxide (ZrO2) was also used by Cioffi and co-workers for supporting palladium NPs by an electrochemical technique. [175] The Pd/ZrO_2 nanocatalyst was demonstrated to be very efficient in Suzuki couplings of aryl bromides and iodides with phenyl boronic acids in water at 90 °C using tetrabutylammonium hydroxide (TBAOH) as a base. It is interesting to note that inorganic bases, such as KOH, $NaHCO_3$, and K_2CO_3, gave unsatisfactory results, thus confirming the advantage of tetrabutylammonium hydroxide in this process. This advantage was most likely derived from the ability of tetrabutylammonium hydroxide to simultaneously function as both a base and a phase transfer agent. The catalyst was also found to be reusable up to ten times without an appreciable loss of activity.

Carbon nanotubes provide a new type of support for catalytic nanoparticles. Because of their small size, carbon nanotubes can be uniformly dispersed in solution, thus increasing contact between the reactants and the catalyst. Attaching metal nanoparticles to carbon nanotubes in aqueous solutions usually requires a tedious procedure; however, a simple method has been reported by Wai et al. that involved depositing metal nanoparticles on the surfaces of multi-walled carbon nanotubes (MWCNTs) by the hydrogen reduction of a Pd(II)-b-diketone precursor in a supercritical carbon dioxide medium. [176] This strategy yielded well-dispersed, spherical particles that were anchored onto the external walls of MWCNTs with a size range of 5–10 nm The catalytic activities of these materials were then studied for Suzuki coupling reactions in methanol. [177] The reaction between phenylboronic acid and 1-iodo-4-nitrobenzene catalyzed by the above catalyst produced nitro-biphenyl with a 94% conversion after 30 min of reaction at 65 °C with a turnover frequency (TOF) of 709 h^{-1}, which is about 24 times greater than commercially available Pd/C catalysts under the same conditions. Later, Corma et al. [178] compared the catalytic activity of three palladium metal-containing single-walled carbon nanotubes (SWNTs) that were prepared by different methodologies to evaluate the importance of particle size in the catalyst for Suzuki cross-couplings.

More recently, functionalized polymers have been used as supports in coupling reactions, and a variety of polymers have proven to be versatile supports due to their potential to combine the easy reuse of heterogeneous catalysts and the high efficiency of homogeneous catalysts.69,70 A study by Sayed et al., [179] detailing Suzuki cross-couplings using polymer supports, reported a series of PVP-stabilised Pd nanoparticles with different Pd particle sizes, prepared using the stepwise growth technique reported by Teranishi et al. [180] Using this method, the authors succeeded in preparing different PVP-Pd composites with a narrow particle size distribution. The turnover frequency (TOF) for the Suzuki reaction between phenylboronic acid and iodobenzene in aqueous solutions was found to depend on the Pd particle size and to exhibit amaximum size of ca. 3.9 nm. A decrease in TOF with increasing particle size means that the reaction is structure-sensitive and involves mainly edge and corner sites. However, the low activity for very small Pd particles can be explained by the strong adsorption of reaction intermediates, which might act as a poison.

The use of dendrimer stabilized metal nanoparticles in catalysis is one of the most important applications of dendrimers. The first examples of the formation of metal nanoparticles stabilized by dendrimers were provided by the groups of Crooks, Tomalia, and Esumi.[181–183] In 2001, El-Sayed and co-workers found that palladium nanoparticles stabilized by hydroxyl-terminated poly(amidoamine) (PAMAM) dendrimers (G3-OH, G represents the generation) could efficiently catalyze the Suzuki–Miyaura reaction between phenylboronic acid or 2-thienylboronic acid and iodobenzene.[184] Using a 1.5 mol% dendrimer Pd solution in refluxing ethanol in the presence of Na_3PO_4 as a base, the desired products were obtained with good to excellent yields

Catalytic systems supported by water-soluble supramolecular receptors have drawn the attention of synthetic chemists because of their outstanding activities, particularly in terms of selectivity. [185,186] Cyclodextrins (CDs) are among the most important molecular receptors studied in supramolecular chemistry. To date, there are relatively few examples of CD-capped Pd nanoparticle catalysts used in Suzuki coupling reactions. Kaifer and co-workers reported the use of perthiolated CDs to cap Pd nanoparticles (Scheme 23). [187] This catalyst has been found to be highly effective in the coupling of aryl iodides at 100 °C using Na_2CO_3 as a base in a mixture of water–acetonitrile (1:1) with 1 mol% of catalyst. However, the coupling of aryl bromides required longer times, and higher catalyst loadings and gave significantly lower yields than aryl iodides.

Catalyst recovery is a vital feature of most of these processes. Although nanocatalysts are highly active, they are not easy to isolate from the reaction mixture, which hampers overall process sustainability. However, the use of magnetic nanoparticles as support (instead of conventional supports like silica or alumina) seems to be a promising option to overcome this separation problem. Because of the paramagnetic character of this support, the synthesized catalysts could also be recovered simply by using an external magnet without a filtration or centrifugation step. Recently, there has been an increasing trend towards the use of magnetically recoverable nanomaterials to develop more efficient and green chemical synthetic processes. [189-190] In addition to their facile separation, these materials have also shown better selectivity, higher activity, and enhanced stability.

8. Catalytic synthesis of Benzimidazole

Benzimidazole [191-197] is conveniently synthesized by the reaction of the corresponding o-phenylenediamine with an acid/aldehyde (Scheme 1.4). This allows the production of a large family of derivatives, including substitution at the 1- or 2-position. Additionally, the benzimidazole ring can be substituted at the 4, 5, 6, or 7-positions, by nitro (1), amino (2), or halogen groups. This not only allows the introduction of other functional groups, which can be used for targeting biomolecules but can have a major effect on the electronic properties, with a consequent influence on the chemical, photochemical and spectroscopic properties.

The literature precedence reveals that the substitution at the 1, 2, 5, and/or 6-positions of the benzimidazole moiety is also crucial from the point of view of medicinal chemistry, to exhibit a wide range of pharmacological activities [198] by acting at different targets. Accordingly, the compounds may be mono-, di- or trisubstituted derivatives of the benzimidazole nucleus. Substitution of an amino group at the 2-position of the benzimidazole pharmacophore is capable of allowing interaction with nucleotidic structures and enzymes, as well as with various enzyme inhibitors. [199] The derivatization at the N–H position of benzimidazole by an electron donating group and substitution with a long chain of propyl, acetamido, thio, thiazole-amino, or tetramethyl piperidine, resulted in good biological activity. [200,201] A 2-phenyl substituent [202] and/or 5-nitro group [203] improved the binding on proteins, through hydrogen bond formation, and/or its electron withdrawing properties, which resulted in p-interactions between the electron deficient ring of the drug and the electron rich ring of the aromatic amino acids. Terminal lipophilic groups are also important for receptor binding affinity, with improved inhibition profiles, solubility, and metabolic stability. [204] Bis-benzimidazole derivatives, with an alkyl chain as a linker, are also important for anticancer activity. [205]

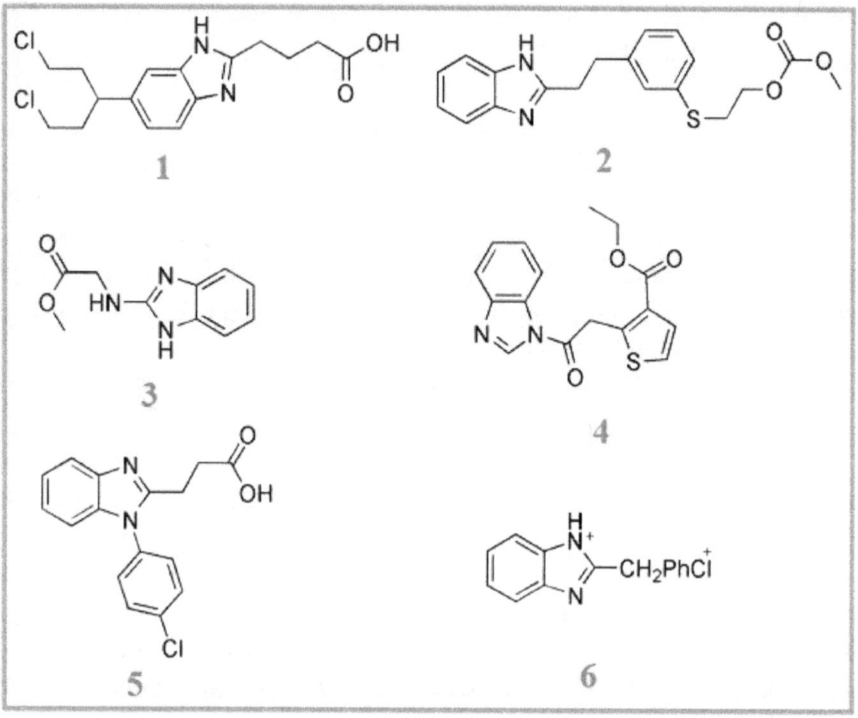

1. Imet 3393 (Anticancer), 2. Bactericide, 3. Carbendazim (Fungicide), 4. Bezitramide (Analgesic), 5. Anti-viral, 6. Diabazole (Vasodilator spasmlytic hypotensive)

The first benzimidazole was prepared by Hoebrecker [206], who obtained 2,5- dimethylbenzimidazole by the reduction and dehydration of 2-nitro-4-methylacetanilide (Scheme 1.4).

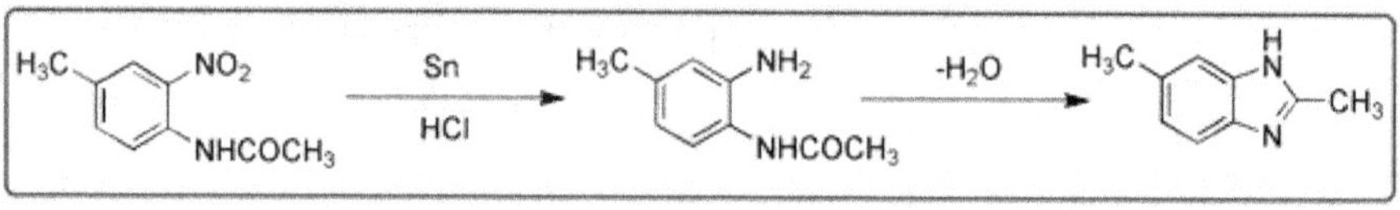

Scheme.1.4. Intricate task of 1,2-disubstutitued benzimidazoles.

However, these methods are usually not suitable limited to the available starting materials. Consequently, improvements were made towards the development of new strategies, such as the metal-catalyzed aryl amination chemistry.

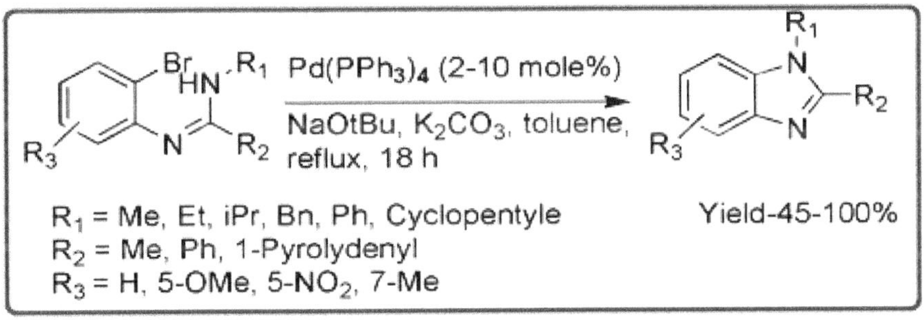

Scheme.1.5. Brain's approach using amidines.[207,208]

The first metal catalyzed intramolecular aryl-amination/cyclization approach was reported by Brain and co-workers,[207, 208] this method was readily adopted with high success by several groups that used several metal salts such as palladium-, copper- or cobalt-based catalysts (Scheme 1.5). In fact, the recent advances in metal-mediated coupling chemistry stimulated the development of these new methodologies, allowing the easy assembly of heterocyclic compounds. Palladium-catalyzed arylamination chemistry has been improved, mainly due to the development of new ligand systems.[209] Concerning copper catalysis, the development of N,N-, N,O-, and O,O-bidentate ligands improved Ullmann-type coupling reactions.[210]

A heretogeneous system for the synthesis of 1,2-disubstituted benzimidazoles using copper(II) oxide nanoparticles under ligand-free conditions was described by Punniyamurthy and co-workers (Scheme 1.6). The reactions were revealed to be efficient and general for the synthesis of 2-alkyl-, 2-aryl-, and 2-aminobenzimidazoles. Moreover, the catalyst could be recovered and recycled without loss of activity and selectivity.[211]

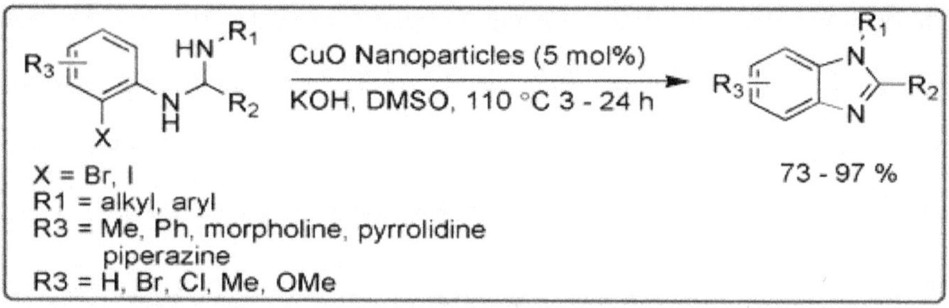

Scheme.1.6. Heterogeneous synthesis of benzimidazoles described by Punniyamurthy.[38]

D. Yang and co-workers, [212] develop an efficient strategy for the synthesis of benzimidazoles. The couplings were performed using readily available starting materials such as o-substituted aminobenzene and various aldehydes in the presence of magnetically separable $CuFe_2O_4$ nanoparticles as the catalyst and dioxygen as the green oxidant, in which $CuFe_2O_4$ nanoparticles could act as a Lewis acid which activates the aldehyde and promote the imine formation and subsequently proceed the aromatization to afford the desired products (scheme.1.7).

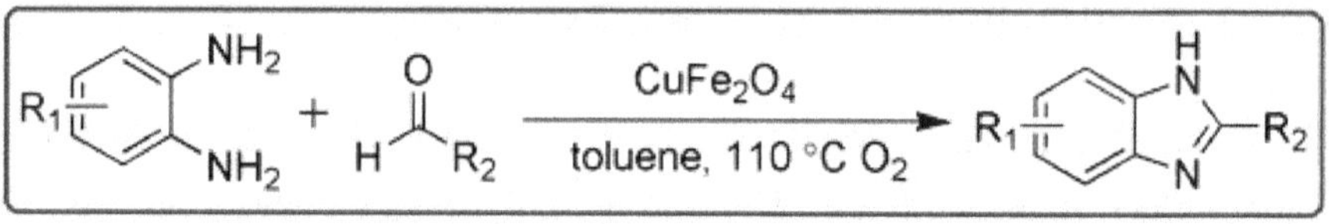

Scheme.1.7. Magnetic $CuFe_2O_4$-catalyzed synthesis of benzoxazoles, benzothiazoles, and benzimidazoles [212]

The benzimidazole derivatives were also synthesized by using mixed oxide nanoparticles in which S. Roy and co-worker [213] described in his work they have synthesize mesoporous TiO_2 -Fe_2O_3 mixed oxide and explored its application in the synthesis of β-amino alcohol and benzimidazole derivatives (scheme.1.8). The mesoporous mixed oxide material showed a good BET (Brunauer–Emmett–Teller theory) surface area, high chemical stability, and excellent catalytic activity. The advantages of this reaction are using a green solvent such as water, high regioselectivity, compatibility of a wide range of functionalities,

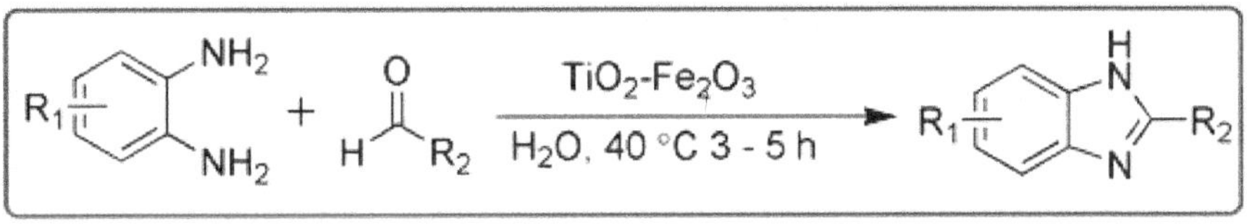

Scheme.1.8. Synthesis of benzimidazoles catalyzed by TiO_2 -Fe_2O_3 mixed oxide [213]

In recent years, many nanomaterials are used to synthesize a variety of fine chemicals such as heterocyclic compounds containing N, O, and S hetero atoms. A. Teimouri and co-worker [214] demonstrate a one-pot, multicomponent methodology for the synthesis of benzimidazoles, benzoxazoles, and benzothiazoles, by the condensation of 1,2-diaminobenzene, 2-aminophenol, or 2-aminothiophenol and substituted aldehydes and the synthesis of quinoxalines derivatives by the condensation of 1,2-diaminobenzene and 1,2-dicarbonyl in ethanol using nano-structured ZnO, nano-sulfated zirconia, nano- -alumina and nano-ZSM-5 zeolites (Zeolite Socony Mobil–5, (scheme.1.9)), as the catalyst.

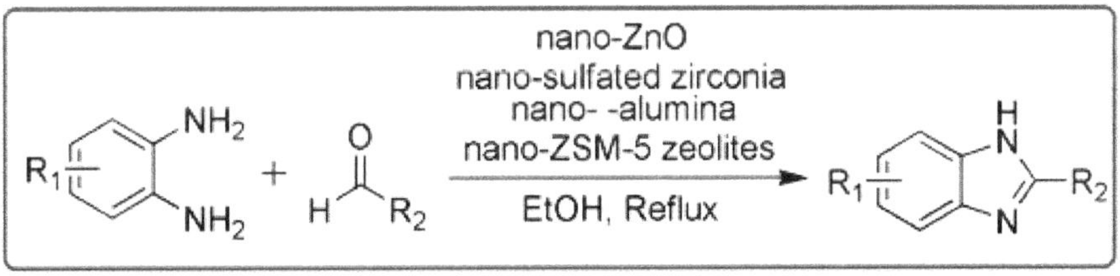

Scheme.1.9. Synthesis of benzimidazoles catalyzed by TiO_2 -Fe_2O_3 mixed oxide

9. Catalytic synthesis of Benzoxazole

N-Heterocyclic compounds are the main building blocks in synthetic organic chemistry and they are often considered privileged target molecules in pharmaceutical industries to develop some activity-specific lead molecules. As a result, the progress in the development of more efficient and versatile methods to synthesize N-heterocycles has always been interesting in organic synthesis. Especially, benzoxazole derivatives have attracted considerable attention because of their wide variety of applications in agrochemicals, natural products, functional materials, and pharmaceutically active molecules [215-217]. The benzoxazole core has been found in a variety of cytotoxic natural products viz., natural antimycobacterial pseudopteroxazole [218,219], UK-1(bisbenzoxazole) [220], AJI9561 [221], and salvianen [222]. On the other hand, it has some medicinal chemistry applications consisting of the cathepsin S inhibitors [223], anticancer agents [224], 5-HT$_3$ receptor agonists (Fig. 1) [225], non-nucleoside HIV reverse transcriptase inhibitors [226], oestrogen receptor-b agonists [227], selective peroxisome proliferator-activated receptor-g antagonists [228], orexin-1 receptor antagonists [229], and elastase inhibitors [230]. In continuation, the benzoxazole core has some other applications such as herbicides, and fenoxaprop, and is also used in fluorescent whitening agents such as bisbenzoxazolyl ethylenes and arenes (Fig. 1) [231]. In contrast, the core of interest has also exhibited remarkable applications in the fields of laser dyes [232], polymer production [233], organic light-emitting diodes (OLEDs) [234], etc. Some of the benzoxazole derivatives, which are already booming in the market, to quote a few, are pseudopteroxazole (antimicrobial agent), UK-1(anticancer agent), AJI9561 (cytotoxic), benoxaprofen (non-steroidal anti-inflammatory drug, NSAID), flunoxaprofen (NSAID), tafamidis (hereditary amyloidosis), salvianen (cytotoxicity) fenoxaprop (herbicide) (Fig. 1.9).

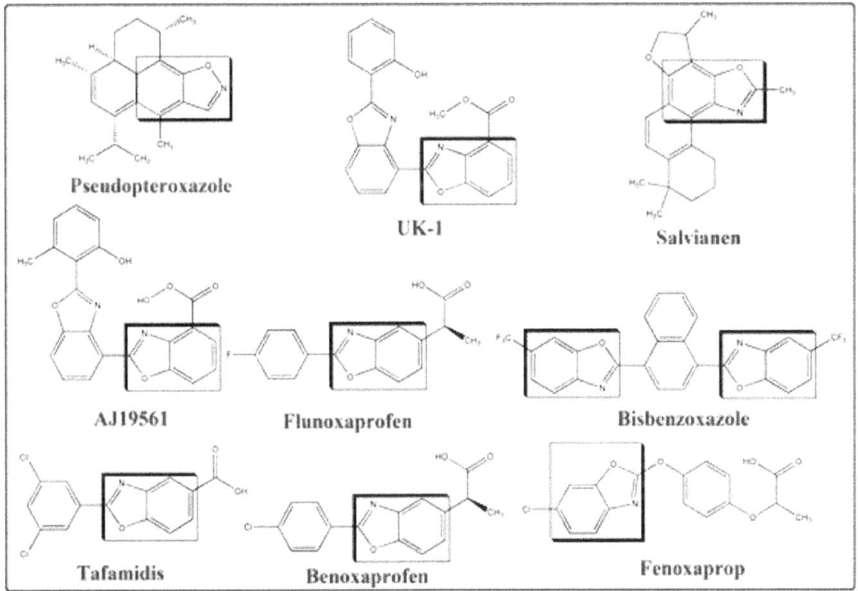

Fig.1.9. Structure of biologically and medicinally active benzoxazole derivatives

Owing to such significance, the synthesis of benzoxazole and its derivatives has been an attractive goal for organic and medicinal chemists. From the literature, it is evident that several synthetic efforts have been made to prepare the benzoxazole scaffold. One of the traditional methods for the synthesis of benzoxazoles involves the construction of the O1-C2 and N3-C2 bonds via condensation of ortho-aminophenol with carboxylic acid or acyl chloride in the presence of a strong acid at elevated temperature [235], and the second widely followed method is through the aldehydes via oxidative cyclization of the phenolic Schiff bases with a wide variety of oxidizing agents viz., $Mn(OAc)_3$ [236], DDQ [237], $ThClO_4$ [238], NiO_2 [239], $ZrOCl_2.8H_2O$ [240], PCC-supported silica gel [241], Dess- Martin reagent [242], $BaMnO_4$ [243], and $Pb(OAc)_4$ [244]. On the other hand, a handful of approaches have been reported for the synthesis of benzoxazoles using diverse catalysts and other reagents viz., silica-supported sodium hydrogen sulfate [245], Indion 190 resin [246], silica sulphuric acid [247], methane sulphonic acid [248], copper triflate [249], Indium triflate [250], $SnCl_2$ [251], $BF_3.OEt_2$ [252], Shvo catalyst {[(η5-Ph_4C_4CO)]$_2HRu_2(CO)_4$(m-

H)}, Co-salen complex, and 2,6-dimethoxybenzoquinone (DMBQ) as the terminal oxidant [253,254]. Yang et al., reported the synthesis of benzoxazole using mesoporous poly(melamine-formaldehyde) as a heterogeneous organocatalyst [255]. Lately, benzoxazole derivatives have also been prepared from 2-aminophenol and aldehydes with activated carbon [256], Pd/C in the presence of Hantzsch ester as a catalyst [257] and Al_3^+ exchanged K-10 clay as a heterogeneous catalyst [258].

Recently, the synthesis of 1,3-benzoxazoles using nanoparticles (NPs) was found to be an eye-catching approach because of their large and reactive surfaces, high potential for selectivity, which may facilitate reaction under milder conditions, shorter reaction time, easier separation of the product, and recyclability of the catalyst [259]. Several metal NPs as catalysts have been reported to synthesize the benzoxazole derivatives viz., CuO NPs supported on silica [260], ZnO NPs [261], nano CeO_2 [262], KCN/ MWCNTs (multi-walled carbon nanotubes) [263] and magnetic copper ferrite NPs [264]. Very recently, Maleki et al. reported the synthesis of benzoxazole derivatives using an Ag@TiO_2 nano composite as a catalyst in aqueous media [265].

10. Graphene oxide decorated metal nanoparticles

Graphene, the novel two-dimensional (2D) material in the carbon family, has stimulated more and more interest since it was first obtained by Geim using a mechanical exfoliation method in 2004 [266], due to its intriguing properties such as high mobility of charge carriers, unique transport performance [267], high mechanical strength [268], and extremely high thermal conductivity and theoretically high surface area of 2600 m^2/g [269]. These fascinating properties render graphene, as a 2D sheet of sp2-hybridized carbon, suitable for many promising applications such as sensors [270], energy conversion devices [271], and catalysts [272]. The large demand for graphene makes the synthesis of graphene one of the key steps to meet various research needs. Micromechanical cleavage of graphite [266], chemical vapour deposition (CVD) [273], reduction of graphite oxide [274], and the graphite intercalation technique [275] are the main methods employed to prepare graphene. Recently, a few novel methods have been reported. Kosynkin et al. have demonstrated a method involving longitudinal unzipping of carbon nanotubes to form graphene nanoribbons [276]. Choucair et al. have shown a method to prepare graphene based on hydrothermal synthesis and sonication [277]. The recent advances in the large-scale synthesis of graphene by CVD on Ni [273,278] and Cu [279,280] films open up various macroscopic applications of graphene.

Moreover, graphene sheets decorated with metal oxide NPs combine their outstanding properties of them and might result in some particular properties because of the synergetic effect between them. The development of graphene-based composites provides an important milestone to improve the application performance of metal oxide nanomaterials in different fields such as energy harvesting, conversion and storage devices, photovoltaic devices, photocatalysis, etc., because the hybrids have versatile and tailor-made properties with performances superior to those of the individual oxide nanomaterials. With this in mind, considerable efforts in decorating graphene with metal oxide NPs [281–283] have recently been reported. To date, various kinds of metal oxides have been synthesized and supported on graphene, which include TiO_2, ZnO, SnO_2, MnO_2, Co_3O_4, Fe_3O_4, Fe_2O_3, NiO, Cu_2O, etc.

The graphite was oxidized by treatment with strong chemical oxidants, such as HNO_3, $KMnO_4$, and H_2SO_4 to form graphite oxide and then graphite oxide was exfoliated into GO sheets in water by ultrasonication to form a stable aqueous dispersion. The GO product can be purified by centrifugation and dialysis to remove aggregates and various inorganic impurities such as metal ions and acids. More importantly, the exfoliated GO sheets usually possess a rich assortment of oxygen-containing groups, such as carboxylic, hydroxyl, and epoxide functional groups. The presence of oxygen functionalities in GO allows interactions with the cations and provides reactive sites for the nucleation and growth of NPs, which result in the rapid growth of various graphene-based composites. Moreover, GO can be reduced to graphene with partial restoration of the sp2-hybridized network by thermal [284], chemical [285], electrochemical [286], photothermal [287], photocatalytic [288], sonochemical [289], and microwave reduction methods [290].

a) Synthesis of graphene oxide decorated metal nanoparticles

In graphene-based composites, graphene acts either as a functional component or a substrate for immobilizing the other components. Here we will mainly focus on recent achievements dealing with the development of effective strategies for synthesizing high-quality graphene–metal oxide composites.

i) Solution mixing method

Solution mixing is an efficient and direct method. It has been widely used to prepare graphene–metal oxide composites. Peak et al. prepared graphene–SnO$_2$ composites by solution mixing [291]. They synthesized SnO$_2$ sol by hydrolysis of SnCl4 with NaOH, and then a graphene dispersion was mixed with the sol in ethylene glycol to form the composites.

Graphene–TiO$_2$ composites were also synthesized following a similar strategy [292]. Commercialized TiO$_2$ NPs (P25) were mixed with Nafion-coated graphene to fabricate dye-sensitized solar cells, where the Nafion served as a 'glue' to tightly bind graphene sheets and P25 [293]. P25 and GO colloids have been mixed ultrasonically, followed by ultraviolet-assisted photocatalytic reduction of GO to yield graphene–TiO$_2$ composites [281]. Akhavan et al. [294] used a similar strategy to prepare the graphene–TiO$_2$ composite thin film.

ii) Sol–gel method

The sol–gel process is a popular approach for the preparation of metal oxide structures and film coatings, with the metal alkoxides or chlorides as precursors that undergo a series of hydrolysis and polycondensation reactions. It has been used to situ prepare TiO$_2$ and Fe$_3$O$_4$ [295–296] nanostructures on graphene sheets. Recently, the Mullen group [297] developed a sol–gel approach to the production of 2D sandwich-like high-quality graphene/mesoporous silica hybrids nanosheets with the aid of cetyltrimethyl ammonium bromide, in which each graphene is fully separated by a mesoporous silica shell (Figure 3). Furthermore, graphene–mesoporous Co$_3$O$_4$ sheets could be prepared using graphene–mesoporous silica sheets as a template by a nanocasting approach. The key advantage of the in situ sol–gel process lies in the fact that the functional groups on GO/RGO (reduced graphene oxide) provide reactive and anchoring sites for nucleation and growth of NPs so that the resulting metal oxide nanostructures are chemically bonded to the GO/RGO surfaces.

iii) Hydrothermal/solvothermal method

Hydrothermal/solvothermal is a powerful tool for the synthesis of inorganic nanocrystals, which operates at an elevated temperature in a confined volume to generate high pressure. The one-pot hydrothermal/ solvothermal process can give rise to nanostructures with high crystallinity without post-synthetic annealing or calcination, and at the same time reduce GO to RGO. A series of graphene–TiO_2 composites were synthesized with a hydrothermal or solvothermal method. Xiang et al. [298] and Jiang et al. [299] reported the synthesis of graphene–TiO_2 composites with exposed {001} high-energy facets by a hydrothermal treatment. Interestingly, graphene–TiO_2 composites with delicately controlled TiO_2 nanostructures, including 12 nm spherical TiO_2–graphene nanosheets (STG), ultra-small 2 nm TiO_2–graphene nanosheets (USTG), and TiO_2 nanorod–graphene nanosheets (NRTG) have been obtained with a one-step solvothermal approach, only by simply adjusting the solvothermal reaction conditions [300]. These methods have been extended to deposit Fe_3O_4, Co_3O_4, and SnO_2 nanostructures on graphene sheets [282,301,302].

iv) Self-assembly

Self-assembly is an efficient and often preferred process to assemble micro- and nano-objects into ordered macroscopic structures [296]. It has been utilized to produce functional materials such as photonic crystals, composites, and ordered DNA structures. In order to obtain the alternating layered structure of the final composites, a novel method has been developed to prepare the ordered graphene–metal oxide hybrids through the surfactant-assisted ternary self-assembly process by Wang et al. [303]. They used an anionic surfactant-modified RGO as the starting material. Surfactant assisted in the dispersal of RGO sheets, and the loading of metal cations. After converting the metal cations to oxides at RGO sheets, graphene–metal oxide composites were obtained with layered structure Alternating layers of RGO-metal oxides, e.g., NiO, SnO2, and MnO2 were prepared by this method. This assembly process is important in constructing layered composite materials.

11. Graphene oxide decorated metal nanoparticles used for photo catalyst dye degradation

Synthetic dyes exhibit considerable structural diversity (Fig. 1.10). The chemical classes of dyes employed more frequently on an industrial scale are the azo, anthraquinone, sulfur, indigoid, triphenylmethyl (trityl), and phthalocyanine derivatives. However, it has to be emphasized that the overwhelming majority of synthetic dyes currently used in the industry are azo derivatives. It should be noted that azoketo hydrazone equilibria can be a vital factor in the easy breakdown of many of the azo dye systems. Some dyes quoted in the review have only marginal importance from the point of view of industrial application.

A wide range of methods has been developed for the removal of synthetic dyes from waters and waste waters to decrease their impact on the environment. The technologies involve adsorption on inorganic or organic matrices, decolorization by photocatalysis, and/or by oxidation processes, microbiological or enzymatic decomposition, etc. [304]. The efficacy of the various methods of dye removal, such as chemical precipitation, chemical oxidation, and adsorption along with their effects on subsequent biological treatment was compared in an earlier paper [305]. Chemical oxidation was very effective but the efficiency was strongly influenced by the type of oxidant.

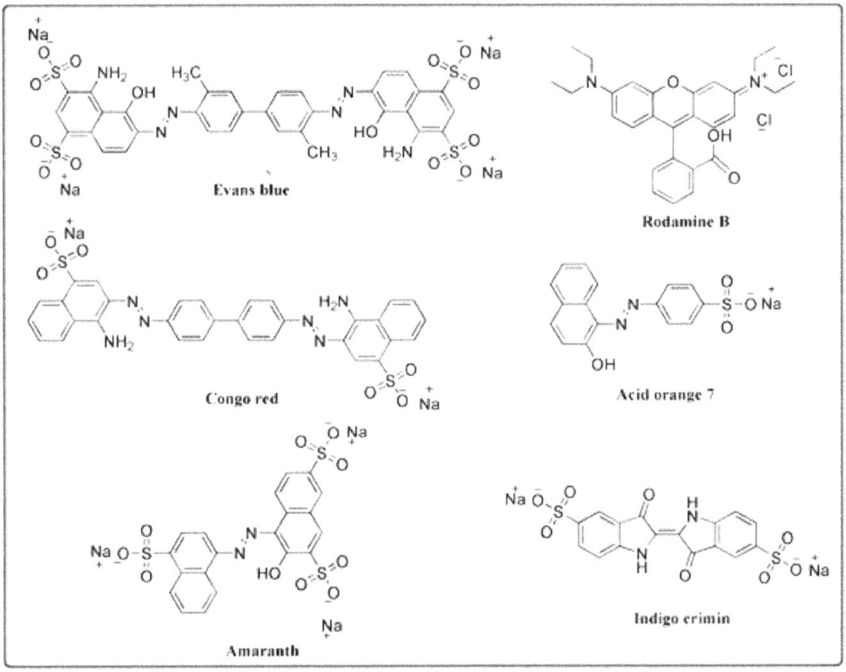

Fig.1.10. The chemical structure of synthetic dyes is most frequently studied in degradation experiments.

A graphene-P25 composite was applied to the photocatalytic degradation of methylene blue [306] in this work demonstrated that the composite of graphene shows a high degree of dye absorptivity, extensive light absorption range, and better charge separation and transportation properties. The author reveals the improved photocatalytic activity in the dye degradation under both UV and visible lights to the two-dimensional conjugated structure of graphene, which facilitated a better platform for dye adsorption and charge transportation.

Chen et al. [307] synthesized $GO-TiO_2$ composites with p/n heterojunction. The GO acts as a p-type semiconductor with a band gap narrower than 2.43 eV, it plays an important role in the visible light photocatalytic performance of $GO-TiO_2$ composites. In which the GO acts as a sensitizer and improves the photocatalytic performance of $GO-TiO_2$ composites in the degradation of methyl orange dye.

Lee et al. [308] reported a low band gap TiO_2 NPs completely wrapped by graphenenin. The graphene-TiO_2 NPs exhibited a red shift of the band edge and a significant reduction of the band gap (2.80 eV), which as a result it enhanced the absorption of visible light. Furthermore, graphene–TiO_2 NPs showed excellent visible light photocatalytic properties for the degradation of methylene blue with a rate constant of 3.41×10^{-2} min^{-1}, which was much higher than that of bare anatase TiO_2 NPs and P25 powder.

CHAPTER TWO

Materials, Methods, and Characterisation Techniques

1. Chemicals

All reagents and starting materials were obtained commercially from Sigma-Aldrich and Merck, himedia, and were used as received without any further purification unless otherwise noted. Freshly distilled solvents were employed for all synthetic purposes. Spectroscopic grade solvents were employed for spectral works. All other chemicals were of AR grade.

2. Purification of the sample

a) Purification of of solvents

Hear in we represent some important organic solvents purification methods we adopted in this work [1,2,3]

Acetone: (BP 56.2) Dry over Molec sieves or K_2CO_3. Removal of aldehydes by $KMnO_4$. High purity: saturate w/ dry NaI, and then chill to -10 C, filter off NaI crystals. Disti sieves. **Acetonitrile:** (BP 81.6) Predry if wet, reflux & stir w/ CaH until gas evolution ceases. Distill and store over sieves.

Benzene: (BP 80.1) Stir w/ H_2SO_4 (.1l/l benzene) and separate acid. Repeat until no darkening occurs, then distill.

Chloroform: (BP 61.2) Shake w/ con H_2SO_4, wash w/ water, dry and distill from K_2CO_3. Alternatively, pass through column of Grade I activated alumina (50g/L solvent).

Diethyl ether: (BP 34.5) Check for peroxides. Pretreat with Na wire, then add LAH (or CaH) and distill.

Ethanol: (BP 78.3) For anhydrous from abs: Reflux 60 ml EtOH, 5 g Mg, and a few drops of CHCl3 or EtBr (catalyst) until all Mg converted to the oxide. Add 900 ml EtO then distill, store over sieves. Abs EtOH can be prepared from 95% if benzene must be excluded (no denaturants if USP grade) by refluxing over CaO fo hours, then distilling.

Ethyl Acetate: (BP 77.1) Wash with 5% Aq Na_2CO_3, then sat. $CaCl_2$; dry over K_2CO_3 and distill from P_2O_5.

Methanol: (BP 64.5) Most water removed by storage over CaO then distillation from CaO. Storage over sieves (NO DRIERITE!!) Ultrapure: 50 ml MeOH, 5 g Mg and 0.5 until I2 color disappears, then add 1 L MeOH and return to reflux 1 h. Distill slowly.

Methylene Chloride: (BP 40.8) Wash with con H_2SO_4, sat. Na_2CO_3, and water. Dry over CaCl2 and distill from P_2O_5. Alternatively, distillation from anhydrous K_2CO_3 and storage ov gives pretty good product.

Dimethyl formamide (DMF) (BP 152) Stir w/ KOH, filter and distill from CaO or BaO.

Dimethyl sulfoxide (DMSO): (BP 189) Dry overnite w/ Drierite, BaO, CaO, or NaOH. Distill from BaO, CaO, or NaOH (2-3mm, 50 C).

b) Purification of organic compounds [1]

Some organic compounds are purified by Simple Crystallisation methods and most of the synthesised organic compounds are purified by Flash Column Chromatography

3. Characterization of the synthesised nanoparticles

a) X-Ray Diffraction Techniques (XRD)

X-ray diffraction (XRD) techniques are useful for revealing structural information of crystalline materials, as these materials cause deflections when illuminated with X-ray. Comprehensive information of the basic principles of the technique and its use for structural analysis can be found in Ladd and Palmer,[4] and Giacovazzo.[5]

XRD samples were prepared by evaporating a drop of nanocrystal solution onto a glass substrate; XRD data were collected using Bruker D8 ADVANCE X-ray diffractometer (CuK radiation) operated at 40 kV and 40 mA over a range of 30-90° by step scanning with a step size of 0.048° at room temperature.

b) Energy Dispersive X-Ray Spectroscopy (EDX)

EDS is a supplementary technique to TEM. It utilises X-rays that are emitted from the atoms in the sample excited by the electron beam to characterise the elemental composition of the analysed volume. In this work, EDS analysis was mainly conducted for ruthenium nanoparticles. EDS spectra were acquired using the The JEOL JSM-7600F analysis [7,8].

c) Transmission Electron Microscopy (TEM)

TEM and TEM-based techniques were the primary characterisation techniques used in this project. These techniques include TEM and high-resolution TEM (HRTEM) imaging, selected area electron diffraction (SAED), and energy-dispersive X-ray spectroscopy (EDS). Each technique is useful for providing certain information about the sample, when combined the techniques become a powerful tool for determining the size, shape, composition, and crystal structure of the materials studied. Detailed information of the basic principles of the TEM and TEM-based techniques, and the applications of these techniques can be found in Williams and Carter [11]. TEM (Transition Electron Microscopy) and selected area electron diffraction (SAED) studies were performed on a Jeol/JEM 2100 operated at 200 KV and magnification is 2000X − 1500000 X.

d) Scanning electron microscopy (SEM)

The TEM is able to study the mesopore structure and crystal structure, however the scanning electron microscope (SEM) is needed to study the three dimensional topography of the PSC material. The SEM can also be used for EDX of the sample [13]. Scanning electron microscopy studies were conducted on an S4800 Scanning Electron Microscope (SEM) and JEOL make and model JSM - 6390LV magnification is 5 × to 300, 000 × (both in high and low vacuum modes)

e) X-ray Photoelectron Microscopy (XPS)

X-ray photoelectron spectroscopy (XPS) was used in this work to analyze chemical state information for the resulting nanoparticles. X-ray photoelectron spectroscopy (XPS) was performed on a Thermo Scientific ESCALAB 250 microprobe with a focused monochromatic Al Kα x-ray (1486.6 eV) source and a 180° hemispherical analyzer with a 6-element multichannel detector and X-ray Photoelectron Spectroscopy (XPS) with Auger Electron Spectroscopy (AES) Module PHI 5000 Versa Prob II, FEI Inc. with a focused monochromatic Al Kα x-ray (1486.6 eV) source and a 180° hemispherical analyzer with a 6-element multichannel detector.

f) Fourier Transform Infrared Spectrometry (FTIR)

Fourier Transform Infrared (FTIR) spectrometry is a complex method of spectroscopy with the ability to identify materials and determine the quality of a sample. This method identifies materials by the "fingerprints" of molecules, as each FTIR spectrum is unique to the measured molecule [23]. In this work we are using FT-IR analysis conducted by using Thermo Nicolet make and Avatar 370 model with the spectral range of 4000-400 cm^{-1}

g) Ultraviolet-Visible Spectroscopy (UV-vis)

The Ultravoilet-Visible Spectroscopy refers to the reflectance or absorption spectroscopy in UVvisible spectral region. It uses the light in visible and adjacent i.e. U.V and near infrared ranges. Molecules undergo electronic transition in this region that is complementary to fluorescence spectroscopy, for UV-Vis spectral analysis we using Varian make and Cary 5000 model with the spectral range of 175 – 3300 nm in addition to this we also use Systronics PC-based double beam UV-Vis spectrophotometer type-2201 range 190 – 1000 nm.

3. Characterization of synthesised catalytic product

a) Melting points

Melting points were measured on a BOETIUS apparatus from PENTAKON Company, Dresden. Melting points were not corrected.

b) Elimental Analysis

The percentage of elements C, H, N, S and O in an organic compound can be individually or simultaneously analyzed over a wide range of sample matrices and concentrations with Elementar Vario EL III instrument.

c) NMR spectra

The ^{1}H NMR spectra were measured at JNM-ECS 400 MHz and ^{13}C NMR on 100 MHz. And Bruker Avance III, 400MHz All measurements were performed at room temperature if not otherwise mentioned. Internal standard was TMS (δ = 0 ppm) or solvent signals recalculated relative to TMS. The multiplicities of ^{13}C NMR signals were determined without coupling constant value with help of gated spectra and/or DEPT 135 experiments. Mulplicity of the signals is given as follows: br. = broad, s = singlet, d = doublet, t = triplet, q = quartet and m = multiplet.

d) liquid chromatographic-mass spectroscopy (LC-MS)

The liquid chromatographic-mass spectroscopy (LC-MS) analysis was performed using a Varian Inc, 410 Prostar Binary LC with 500 MS IT PDA Detectors.

CHAPTER THREE

Reference

1. Moores, F. Goettmann, *New J. Chem.*, **2006**, 30, 8, 1121.
2. M.-C. Daniel, D. Astruc, *Chem. Rev.*, **2004**, 104, 1, 293.
3. J. D. Aiken III, R. G. Finke, *J. Mol. Catal. A*, **1999**, 145, 1–2, 1.
4. J. Hu, T. W. Odom, C. M. Lieber, *Acc. Chem. Res.* **1999**, *32*, 435.
5. Y. Xia, P. Yang, Y. Sun, Y. Wu, B. Mayer, B. Gates, Y. Yin, F. Kim, H. Yan, *Adv. Mater.* **2003**, *15*, 353.
6. M. Law, J. Goldberger, P. Yang, *Annu. Rev. Mater. Res.* **2004**, 34, 83.
7. A. P. H. J. Schenning, E. W. Meijer, *Chem. Commun.* **2005**, 3245.
8. Y. Li, F. Qian, J. Xiang, C. M. Lieber, *Materials Today*, **2006**, 9, 18.
9. W. Lu, C. M. Lieber, *Nat. Mater.*, **2007**, 6, 841.
10. A. Facchetti, *Materials Today*, **2007**, 10, 28.
11. A. de la Escosura, M. V. Martinez-Diaz, P. Thordarson, A. E. Rowan, R. J. M. Nolte, T. Torres, *J. Am. Chem. Soc.* **2003**, 125, 12300.
12. F. Yang, M. Shtein, S. R. Forrest, *Nat. Mater.* **2005**, 4, 37.
13. Q. Tang, H. Li, M. He, W. Hu, C. Liu, K. Chen, C. Wang, Y. Liu, D. Zhu, *Adv. Mater.* **2006**, 18, 65.
14. W. Y. Tong, A. B. Djurisic, M. H. Xie, A. C. M. Ng, K. Y. Cheung, W. K. Chan, Y. H. Leung, H. W. Lin, S. Gwo, *J. Phys. Chem. B*, **2006**, 110, 17406.
15. L. Schmidt-Mende, A. Fechtenkötter, K. Müllen, E. Moons, R. H. Friend, J. D. MacKenzie, *Science.* **2001**, 293, 1119.
16. A. P. H. J. Schenning, J. v. Herrikhuyzen, P. Jonkheijm, Z. Chen, F. Würthner, E. W. Meijer, *J. Am. Chem. Soc.* **2002**, 124, 10252.
17. K. Sugiyasu, N. Fujita, S. Shinkai, *Angew. Chem. Int. Ed.* **2004**, 43, 1229.
18. H. Liu, Y. Li, S. Xiao, H. Gan, T. Jiu, H. Li, L. Jiang, D. Zhu, D. Yu, B. Xiang, Y. Chen, *J. Am. Chem. Soc.* **2003**, 125, 10794.
19. Y. Sakamoto, T. Suzuki, M. Kobayashi, Y. Gao, Y. Fukai, Y. Inoue, F. Sato, S. Tokito, *J. Am. Chem. Soc.* **2004**, 126, 8138.

20. X. Zhang, X. Zhang, W. Shi, X. Meng, C. Lee, S. Lee, *J. Phys. Chem. B* **2005**, *109*, 18777-18780; d) A. L. Briseno, S. C. B. Mannsfeld, X. Lu, Y. Xiong, S. A. Jenekhe, Z. Bao, Y. Xia, *Nano Lett.* **2007**, 7, 668.

21. C. Barrett, D. Iacopino, D. O'Carroll, G. De Marzi, D. A. Tanner, A. J. Quinn, G. Redmond, *Chem. Mater.* **2007**, *19*, 338-340.

22. Y. Sun, K. Ye, H. Zhang, J. Zhang, L. Zhao, B. Li, G. Yang, B. Yang, Y. Wang, S.-W. Lai, C.-M. Che, *Angew. Chem. Int. Ed.* **2006**, *45*, 5610-5613; *Angew. Chem.* **2006**, *118*, 5738-5741;

23. W. Lu, V. A. L. Roy, C.-M. Che, *Chem. Commun.* **2006**, 3972-3974;

24. M.-Y. Yuen, V. A. L. Roy, W. Lu, S. C. F. Kui, G. S. M. Tong, M.-H. So, S. S.-Y. Chui, M. Muccini, J. Q. Ning, S. J. Xu, C.-M. Che, *Angew. Chem. Int. Ed.* **2008**, *47*, 9895-9899; *Angew. Chem.* **2008**, *120*, 10043-10047.

25. For reviews, see: a) J.-C. Chambron, V. Heitz, J.-P. Sauvage, in *The Porphyrin Handbook*, Vol. 6 (Eds: K. M. Kadish, K. M. Smith, R. Guilard), Academic Press, New York **2000**, pp 1-42;

26. J.-H. Chou, M. E. Kosal, H. S. Nalwa, N. A. Rakow, K. S. Suslick, in *The Porphyrin Handbook*, Vol. 6 (Eds: K. M. Kadish, K. M. Smith, R. Guilard), Academic Press, New York **2000**, pp 43-131.

27. X. Gong, T. Milic, C. Xu, J. D. Batteas, C. M. Drain, *J. Am. Chem. Soc.* **2002**, *124*, 14290-14291.

28. A. D. Schwab, D. E. Smith, C. S. Rich, E. R. Young, W. F. Smith, J. C. de Paula, *J. Phys. Chem. B* **2003**, *107*, 11339-11345;

29. A. D. Schwab, D. E. Smith, B. Bond-Watts, D. E. Johnston, J. Hone, A. T. Johnson, J. C. de Paula, W. F. Smith, *Nano Lett.* **2004**, *4*, 1261-1265;

30. S. C. Doan, S. Shanmugham, D. E. Aston, J. L. McHale, *J. Am. Chem. Soc.* **2005**, *127*, 5885-5892;

31. L. M. Scolaro, A. Romeo, M. A. Castriciano, N. Micali, *Chem. Commun.* **2005**, 3018-3020.

32. Z. Wang, C. J. Medforth, J. A. Shelnutt, *J. Am. Chem. Soc.* **2004**, *126*, 15954-15955;

33. Z. Wang, C. J. Medforth, J. A. Shelnutt, *J. Am. Chem. Soc.* **2004**, *126*, 16720-16721;

34. J.-S. Hu, Y.-G. Guo, H.-P. Liang, L.-J. Wan, L. Jiang, *J. Am. Chem. Soc.* **2005**, *127*, 17090-17095;

35. T. Kojima, R. Harada, T. Nakanishi, K. Kaneko, S. Fukuzumi, *Chem. Mater.* **2007**, *19*, 51-58.

36. A. P. H. J. Schenning, F. B. G. Benneker, H. P. M. Geurts, X. Y. Liu, R. J. M. Nolte, *J. Am. Chem. Soc.* **1996**, *118*, 8549-8552;

37. A. P. H. J. Schenning, E. W. Meijer, F. C. de Schryver, R. J. M. Nolte, *J. Am. Chem. Soc.* **1998**, *120*, 11054-11060;

38. H. A. M. Biemans, A. E. Rowan, A. Verhoeven, P. Vanoppen, L. Latterini, J. Foekema, A. P. H. J. Schenning, E. W. Meijer, F. C. de Schryver, R. J. M. Nolte, *J. Am. Chem. Soc.* **1998**, *120*, 11054-11060;

39. C. R. L. P. N. Jeukens, M. C. Lensen, F. J. P. Wijnen, J. A. A. W. Elemans, P. C. M. Christianen, A. E. Rowan, J. W. Gerritsen, R. J. M. Nolte, J. C. Maan, *Nano Lett.* **2004**, *4*, 1401-1406;

40. M. C. Lensen, K. Takazawa, J. A. A. W. Elemans, C. R. L. P. N. Jeukens, P. C. M. Christianen, J. C. Maan, A. E. Rowan, R. J. M. Nolte, *Chem. Eur. J.* **2004**, *10*, 831-839.

41. M. A. Baldo, D. F. O'Brien, Y. You, A. Shoustikov, S. Sibley, M. E. Thompson, S. R. Forrest, *Nature*, **1998**, *395*, 151-154.

42. Z. Wang, Z. Li, C. J. Medforth, J. A. Shelnutt, *J. Am. Chem. Soc.* **2007**, *129*, 2440-2441.

43. R. Rotomskis, R. Augulis, V. Snitka, R. Valiokas, B. Liedberg, *J. Phys. Chem. B* **2004**, *108*, 2833-2838; b) M. A. Castriciano, A. Romeo, V. Villari, N. Micali, L. M. Scolaro, *J. Phys. Chem. B* **2004**, *108*, 9054-9059.

44. J. A. A. W. Elemans, R. van Hameren, R. J. M. Nolte, A. E. Rowan, *Adv. Mater.* **2006**, *18*, 1251-1266.

45. C. Burda, X. Chen, R. Narayanan, M. A. El-Sayed, *Chem. Rev.* **2005**, *105*, 1025-1102 and references therein;

46. *The Chemistry of Nanomaterials: Synthesis, Properties and Applications*, Vol. 1 & 2, (Eds: C. N. R. Rao, A. Muller, A. K. Cheetham), Wiley-VCH, Weinheim **2004**.

47. T. D. Brennan, W. R. Scheidt, J. A. Shelnutt *J. Am. Chem. Soc.* **1988**, *110*, 3919-3924;

48. R. Pak, W. R. Scheidt, *Acta Crystallogr. C* **1991**, *47*, 431-433; c) A. Ozarowski, H. M. Lee, A. L. Balch, *J. Am. Chem. Soc.* **2003**, *125*, 12606-12614.

49. Y.-Y. Noh, J.-J. Kim, Y. Yoshida, K. Yase, *Adv. Mater.* **2003**, *15*, 699-702;

50. Y.-Y. Noh, J.-J. Kim, K. Yase, S. Nagamatsu, *Appl. Phys. Lett.* **2003**, *83*, 1243-1245;

51. C.-M. Che, H.-F. Xiang, S. S.-Y. Chui, Z.-X. Xu, V. A. L. Roy, J. J. Yan, W.-F. Fu, P. T. Lai, I. D. Williams, *Chem. Asian J.* **2008**, *3*, 1092-1103.

52. Y. Shao, Y. Yang, *Adv. Mater.* **2005**, *17*, 2841-2844.

53. P. O'Brien, N. Pickett, in *The Chemistry of Nanomaterials: Synthesis, Properties and Applications*, Vol. 1 (Eds: C. N. R. Rao, A. Muller, A. K.

Cheetham), Wiley-VCH, Weinheim **2004**, pp 12-30.

54. G. M. Godziela, H. M. Goff, *J. Am. Chem. Soc.* **1986**, *108*, 2237-2243.

55. J. W. Buchler, L. Puppe, *Leibigs Ann. Chem.* **1974**, 1046-1062.

56. E. B. Fleischer, A. Laszlo, *Inorg. Nucl. Chem. Lett.* **1969**, *5*, 373-376;

57. C.-M. Che, R. W.-Y. Sun, W.-Y. Yu, C.-B. Ko, N. Zhu, H. Sun, *Chem. Commun.* **2003**, 1718-1719;

58. R. W. Y. Sun, Ph.D. thesis, The University of Hong Kong, Hong Kong SAR, China, **2004**;

59. Y. Wang, Q.-Y. He, R. W.-Y. Sun, C.-M. Che, J.-F. Chiu, *Cancer Res.* **2005**, *65*, 11553-11564.

60. Xia, Y.; Xiong, Y.; Lim, B.; Skrabalak, S. E. Shape-Controlled Synthesis of Metal Nanocrystals: Simple Chemistry Meets Complex Physics? Angew. Chem., Int. Ed. 2009, 48, 60–103.

61. Tao, A. R.; Habas, S.; Yang, P. Shape Control of Colloidal Metal Nanocrystals. Small 2008, 4, 310–325.

62. DeSantis, C. J.; Skrabalak, S. E. Core Values: Elucidating the Role of Seed Structure in the Synthesis of Symmetrically Branched Nanocrystals. J. Am. Chem. Soc. 2013, 135, 10–13.

63. Mulvihill, M. J.; Ling, X. Y.; Henzie, J.; Yang, P. Anisotropic Etching of Silver Nanoparticles for Plasmonic Structures Capable of Single-Particle SERS. J. Am. Chem. Soc. 2010, 132, 268–274.

64. Kim, D. Y.; Yu, T.; Cho, E. C.; Ma, Y.; Park, O. O.; Xia, Y. Synthesis of Gold Nano-hexapods with Controllable Arm Lengths and Their Tunable Optical Properties. Angew. Chem., Int. Ed. 2011, 50, 6328 6331.

65. Maksimuk, S.; Teng, X.; Yang, H. Roles of Twin Defects in the Formation of Platinum Multipod Nanocrystals. J. Phys. Chem. C 2007, 111, 14312–14319.

66. Wang, L.; Yamauchi, Y. Autoprogrammed Synthesis of Triple- Layered Au@Pd@Pt Core-Shell Nanoparticles Consisting of a Au@Pd Bimetallic Core and Nanoporous Pt Shell. J. Am. Chem. Soc. 2010, 132, 13636–13638.

67. Kobayashi, H.; Lim, B.; Wang, J.; Camargo, P. H. C.; Yu, T.; Kim, M. J.; Xia, Y. Seed- Mediated Synthesis of Pd–Rh Bimetallic Nanodendrites. Chem. Phys. Lett. 2010, 494, 249–254.

68. Lee, Y. W.; Kim, M.; Kim, Y.; Kang, S. W.; Lee, J.-H.; Han, S. W. Synthesis and Electrocatalytic Activity of Au–Pd Alloy Nanodendrites for Ethanol Oxidation. J. Phys. Chem. C 2010, 114, 7689–7693.

69. Lim, B.; Jiang, M.; Camargo, P. H. C.; Cho, E. C.; Tao, J.; Lu, X.; Zhu, Y.; Xia, Y. Pd-Pt Bimetallic Nanodendrites with High Activity for Oxygen Reduction. Science 2009, 324, 1302–1305.

70. Zhang, Q.; Lee, I.; Joo, J. B.; Zaera, F.; Yin, Y. Core-Shell Nanostructured Catalysts. Acc. Chem. Res. 2013, 46, 1816–1824.

71. Skrabalak, S. E.; Xia, Y. Pushing Nanocrystal Synthesis toward Nanomanufacturing. ACS Nano 2009, 3, 10–15.

72. DeSantis, C. J.; Weiner, R. G.; Radmilovic, A.; Bower, M. M.; Skrabalak, S. E. Seeding Bimetallic Nanostructures as a New Class of Plasmonic Colloids. J. Phys. Chem. Lett. 2013, 4, 3072–3082.

73. Liakakos, N.; Cormary, B.; Li, X.; Lecante, P.; Respaud, M.; Maron, L.; Falqui, A.; Genovese, A.; Vendier, L.; Koïnis, S.; Chaudret, B.; Soulantica, K. The Big Impact of a Small Detail: Cobalt Nanocrystal Polymorphism as a Result of Precursor Addition Rate during Stock Solution Preparation. J. Am. Chem. Soc. 2012, 134, 17922–17931.

74. Cotton, F. A.; Wilkinson, G.; Murillo, C. A.; Bochmann, M. Advanced Inorganic Chemistry, 6th ed.; Wiley-Interscience: New York, 1999.

75. Hutchison, J. E. Greener Nanoscience: A Proactive Approach to Advancing Applications and Reducing Implications of Nanotechnology. ACS Nano 2008, 2, 395–402.

76. Cormary, B.; Dumestre, F.; Liakakos, N.; Soulantica, K.; Chaudret, B. Organometallic Precursors of Nano-Objects, A Critical View. Dalton Trans. 2013, 42, 12546–12553.

77. M. Brust, M. Walker, D. Bethell, D. J. Schiffrin and R. Whyman, *J. Chem. Soc., Chem. Commun.*, 1994,(7), 801

78. B. P. S. Chauhan, J. S. Rathore and T. Bandoo, *J. Am. Chem. Soc.*, 2004, **126**, (27), 8493

79. S. Y. Lee, M. Yamada and M. Miyake, *Sci. Technol. Adv. Mater.*, 2005, **6**, (5), 420

80. F. Lu, J. Ruiz and D. Astruc, *Tetrahedron Lett.*, 2004, **45**, (51), 9443

81. J. Alvarez, J. Liu, E. Román and A. E. Kaifer, *Chem. Commun.*, 2000, (13), 1151

82. W. W. Weare, S. M. Reed, M. G. Warner and J. E. Hutchison, *J. Am. Chem. Soc.*, 2000, **122**, (51), 12890

83. M. Tamura and H. Fujihara, *J. Am. Chem. Soc.*, 2003, **125**, (51), 15742

84. S. U. Son, Y. Jang, K. Y. Yoon, E. Kang and T. Hyeon, *Nano Lett.*, 2004, **4**, (6), 1147

85. A. A. Athawale, S. V. Bhagwat, P. P. Katre, A. J. Chandwadkar and P. Karandikar, *Mater. Lett.*, 2003, **57**, (24–25), 3889

86. T. Mayer-Gall, A. Birkner and G. Dyker, *J. Organomet. Chem.*, 2008, **693**, (1), 1

87. C. J. Serpell, J. Cookson, D. Ozkaya and P. D. Beer, *Nature Chem.*, 2011, **3**, (6), 478

88. D. I. Gittins and F. Caruso, *Angew. Chem. Int. Ed.*, 2001, **40**, (16), 3001

89. J. Huang, T. Jiang, B. Han, H. Gao, Y. Chang, G. Zhao, W. Wu, *Chem. Commun.*, 2003, 1654–1655

90. D. Ganapathy, G. Sekar, Catal. Commun. 2013, 39, 50–54.

91. V. K. R. Kumar, K. R. Gopidas, Tetrahedron Lett. 2011, 52, 3102–3105.

92. T. Mayer-Gall, A. Birkner, G. Dyker, J. Organomet. Chem. 693 (2008) 1–3

93. M. Singla, S. C. Mohapatra, S. Ahmad, Mater. Chem. Phys. 137 (2012) 118-128

94. D. G. Galvez, P. Nolis, K. Philippot, B. Chaudret, P. W. N. M. van Leeuwen, ACS Catal. 2012, 2, 317–321

95. W. Niu, G. Xu. Nano Today, 2011, 6: 265–285

96. C. J. Murphy, A. M. Gole, S. E. Hunyadi, C. J. Orendorff. Inorg Chem, 2006, 45: 7544–7554

97. J. X. Gao, C. M. Bender, C. J. Murphy. *Langmuir*, 2003, 19: 9065–9070

98. C. J. Murphy, T. K. San, A. M. Gole, C. J. Orendorff, J. X. Gao, L. Gou, S. E. Hunyadi, T. Li. *J Phys Chem B*, 2005, 109: 13857–13870

99. N. R. Jana, L. Gearheart, C. J. Murphy. *Chem. Mater*, 2001, 13: 2313–2322

100. K. R. Brown, M. J. Natan, Langmuir 1998, 14, 726.

101. N. R. Jana, L. Gearheart, C. J. Murphy, Langmuir 2001, 17, 6782.

102. N. R. Jana, L. Gearheart, C. Murphy, J. Chem. Mater. 2001, 13,

103. K. Mallick, Z. L. Wang, T. Pal, J. Photochem. Photobiol., A. 2001, 140, 75

104. T. K. Sau, A. Pal, N. R. Jana, Z. L. T. Wang, Pal, J. Nanopart. Res. 2001, 3, 257.

105. N. R. Jana, Z. L. Wang, T. K. Sau, T. Pal, Curr. Sci. 2000, 79, 1367.

106. X. Huang, S. Tang, B. Liu, B. Ren, N. Zheng, Adv. Mater., 2011, 23, 3420–3425;

107. J. Gong, F. Zhou, Z. Li and Z. Tang, Chem. Commun., 2013, 49, 4379-4381;

108. L. Chen, B. Huang, X. Qiu, Xi. Wang, R. Luque, Y. Li, **Chem. Sci.**, 2016, **7**, 228-233

109. A. Mayence, M. Wery, D. T. Tran, E. Wetterskog, P. Svedlindh, C. W. Tai, L. Bergstroma, *Nanoscale*, 2016,**8**, 14171-14177

110. S. Wang, L. Lu, M. Yang, Y. Lei, G. Shen, R. Yu, Analytica Chimica Acta 651 (2009) 220–226

111. R. Sivakumar, K. Punitha, C. Sanjeeviraja, R. Gopalakrishnan, Materials Letters 121 (2014) 141–144

112. Jun, Y. W., Seo, J.-W., & Cheon, J. (2008). Acc. Chem. Res. , 41 (2), 179-189.

113. Lu, A.-H., Salabas, E., & Schüth, F. (2007). Angew. Chem. Int. Ed. 46 , 1222-1244.

114. Gubin, S., Koksharov, Y. A., Khomutov, G., & Yu., Y. G. (2005). Russ. Chem. Rev. , 74(6), 489-520.

115. Y. Zhang, Z. Yang, D. Yin, Y. Liu, C. Fei, R. Xiong, J. Shi, G. Yan, **322**(2010)3470

116. Z. Zi, Y. Sun, X. Zhu, Z. Yang, J. Dai, W. Song, **321**(2009)1251

117. I. Sharifi, H. Shokrollahi, M. M. Doroodmand, R. Safi, **324**(2012)1854

118. M. G. Naseri, E. B. Saion, H. A. Ahangar, A. H. Shaari, M. Hashim, *"Nanomaterials"*, DOI:10.1155/2010/907686

119. Y. Kim, D. Kim, C. S. Lee, *"Physica B"*, **337**(2003)42

120. K. Hedayati, S. Azarakhsh, D. Ghanbari, *"DOI:10.7508/ jns.2016.02.004"*(2016)125

121. F. Huixia, C. Baiyi, Z. Devi, J. T. Lin, *"Magnetism and Magnetic Materials"*, **356**(2014)68

122. J. Chen, Z. H. Lu, Y. Wang, X. Chen, L. Zhang Int. J. Hydrogen Energy 40 (2015) 4777-4785

123. M. Kaya, M. Zahmakiran, S. O. zkar, M. R Volkan, ACS Appl. Mater. Interfaces 2012, 4, 3866–3873

124. R. S. Gaikwad, S. Y. Chae, R. S. Mane, S. H. Han, O. S. Joo, International Journal of Electrochemistry Volume 2011, Article ID 729141, 6 pages doi:10.4061/2011/729141

125. V. Polshettiwar, R. Luque, A. Fihri, H. Zhu, M. Bouhrara, J. -M. Basset, *Chem. Rev.* **2011**, *111*, 3036–3075.

126. A. H. Lu, E. L. Salabas, F. Schuth, *Angew. Chem. Int. Ed.* **2007**, *46*, 1222–1244.

127. M. J. Jacinto, P. K. Kiyohara, S. H. Masunaga, R. F. Jardim, L. M. Rossi, *Appl. Catal. A-Gen.* **2008**, *338*, 52–57.

128. S. P. Gubin (ed.), *Magnetic Nanoparticles*, Wiley VCH Weinheim, **2009**.

129. A. H. Lu, W. Schmidt, N. Matoussevitch, H. Bönnemenn, B. Spliethoff, B. Tesche, E. Bill, W. Kiefer, F. Schüth, *Angew. Chem. Int. Ed.* **2004**, *43*, 4303–4306.

130. L. M. Rossi, F. P. Silva, L. L. R. Vono, P. K. Kiyohara, E. L. Duarte, R. Itri, R. Landers, G. Machado, *Green Chem.* **2007**, *9*, 379–385.

131. A. Hu, G. T. Yee, W. Lin, *J. Am. Chem. Soc.* **2005**, *127*, 12486–12487.

132. V. Polshettiwar, R. S. Varma, *Chem. Eur. J.* **2009**, *15*, 1582–1586.

133. B. Baruvati, V. Polshettiwar, R. S. Varma, *Tetrahedr. Lett.* **2009**, *50*, 1215–1218.

134. Handbook of Organopalladium Chemistry for Organic Synthesis; Negishi, E.-I., de Meijere, A., Eds.; Wiley-VCH: Weinheim, Germany, 2002.

135. Metal-Catalyzed Cross-Coupling Reactions, 2nd ed.; de Meijere, A., Diederich, F., Eds.; Wiley-VCH: Weinheim, Germany, 2008.

136. Torborg, C.; Beller, M. Recent Applications of Palladium-Catalyzed Coupling Reactions in the Pharmaceutical, Agrochemical, and Fine Chemical Industries. Adv. Synth. Catal. 2009, 351, 3027–3043.

137. Magano, J.; Dunetz, J. R. Large-Scale Applications of Transition Metal-Catalyzed Couplings for the Synthesis of Pharmaceuticals. Chem. Rev. 2011, 111, 2177–2250.

138. Nanoparticles and Catalysis; Astruc, D., Ed.; Wiley-VCH: New York, 2008.

139. Zahmakıran, M.; Ozkar, S. Metal Nanoparticles in Liquid Phase Catalysis: from Recent Advances to Future Goals. Nanoscale 2011, 3, 3462–3481.

140. Beletskaya P., I.; Cheprakov V., A. The Heck Reaction as a Sharpening Stone of Palladium Catalysis. *Chem. Rev.* **2000**, *100*, 3009.

141. Espinet, P.; Echavarren, A. M. The mechanisms of the Stille reaction. *Angewandte Chemie - International Edition*, 2004, *43*, 4704–4734.

142. Miyaura, N.; Suzuki, A. Palladium-Catalyzed Cross-Coupling Reactions of Organoboron Compounds. *Chem. Rev.* **1995**, *95*, 2457.

143. Knowles, J. P.; Whiting, A. The Heck-Mizoroki cross-coupling reaction: a mechanistic perspective. *Org. Biomol. Chem.* **2007**, *5*, 31.

144. M. Beller, H. Fischer, K. Ku¨hlein, C. P. Reisinger and W. A. Herrmann, J. Organomet. Chem., 1996, 520, 257.

145. M. T. Reetz and G. Lohmer, Chem. Commun., 1996, 1921;

146. M. T. Reetz, E. Westermann, R. Lohmer and G. Lohmer, Tetrahedron Lett., 1998, 39, 8449;

147. J. Le Bars, U. Specht, J. S. Bradley and D. G. Blackmond, Langmuir, 1999, 15, 7621.

148. A. Gniewek, A. M. Trzeciak, J. J. Zio´lkowsky, L. Kepinski, J. Wrzyszcz and W. Tylus, J. Catal., 2005, 229, 332.

149. L. Li, L. X. Zhang, J.-L. Shi, J.-N. Yan and J. Liang, Appl. Catal., A, 2005, 283, 85;

150. C. C. Cassol, A. P. Umpierre, G. Machado, S. I. Wolke and J. Dupont, J. Am. Chem. Soc., 2005, 127, 3298.

151. J. Guerra and M. A. Herrero, Nanoscale, 2010, 2, 1390 and references therein.

152. A. R. Siamaki, A. R. S. Khder, V. Abdelsayed, M. S. El-Shall and B. F. Gupton, J. Catal., 2011, 279, 1.

153. U. Laska, C. G. Frost, G. J. Price and P. K. Plucinski, J. Catal., 2009, 268, 318

154. V. Farina, Adv. Synth. Catal., 2004, 346, 1553;

155. J.-L. Malleron, J.-C. Fiaud and J.-Y. Legros, Hand book of Palladium Catalyzed Organic Reactions: Synthetic Aspects and Catalytic Cycles; Academic Press: San Diego, 1997;

156. J.-C. Hierso, M. Beauperin and P. Meunier, Eur. J. Inorg. Chem., 2007, 3760.

156.

157. N. Miyaura and A. Suzuki, Chem. Rev., 1995, 95, 2457

158. G. A. Molander and B. Canturk, Org. Lett., 2008, 10, 2135.

158.

159. N. Miyaura, K. Yamada and A. Suzuki, Tetrahedron Lett., 1979, 10 20, 3437

160. N. Miyaura and A. Suzuki, J. Chem. Soc. Chem. Commun., 1979, 866.

161. S. Budagumpi, R. A. Haque and A. W. Salman, Coord. Chem. Rev., 2012, 256, 1787;

162. E. A. B. Kantchev, C. J. O'Brien and M. G. Organ, Angew. Chem. Int. Ed., 2007, 46, 2768;

163. T. Ishiyama, S. Abe, N. Miyaura and A. Suzuki, Chem. Lett., 1992, 691

164. J. Zhou and G. C. Fu, J. Am. Chem. Soc., 2004, 126, 1340;

165. A. J. J. Lennox and G. C. Lloyd-Jones, Chem. Soc. Rev., 2014, 43, 412

166. G. A. Molander and B. Canturk, Org. Lett., 2008, 10, 2135.

167. Balanta, A.; Godard, C.; Claver, C. Pd Nanoparticles for C–C Coupling Reactions. Chem. Soc. Rev. 2011, 40, 4973–4985.

168. Fihri, A.; Bouhrara, M.; Nekoueishahraki, B.; Basset, J.-M.; Polshettiwar, V. Nanocatalysts for Suzuki Cross-Coupling Reactions. Chem. Soc. Rev. 2011, 40, 5181–5203.

169. D. E. De Vos, M. Dams, B. F. Sels and P. A. Jacobs, Chem. Rev., 2002, 102, 3615.

170. V. Polshettiwar and A. Molnar, Tetrahedron, 2007, 63, 6949.

171. V. Polshettiwar, C. Len and A. Fihri, Coord. Chem. Rev., 2009, 253, 2599.

172. P. Han, X. Wang, X. Qiu, X. Ji and L. Gao, J. Mol. Catal. A: Chem., 2007, 272, 136.

173. Z. Chen, Z.-M. Cui, F. Niu, L. Jiang and W.-G. Song, Chem. Commun., 2010, 46, 6524.

174. M. L. Kantam, S. Roy, M. Roy, B. Sreedhar, B. M. Choudary, Adv. Synth. Catal., 2005, 347, 2002.

175. A. Monopoli, A. Nacci, V. Calo`, F. Ciminale, P. Cotugno, A. Mangone, L. C. Giannossa, P. Azzone and N. Cioffi, Molecules, 2010, 15, 4511.

176. X. R. Ye, Y. Lin and C. M. Wai, Chem. Commun., 2003, 642.

177. H. B. Pan, C. H. Yen, B. Yoon, M. Sato and C. M. Wai, Synth. Commun., 2006, 36, 3473.

178. A. Corma, H. Garcia and A. Leyva, J. Mol. Catal. A: Chem., 2005, 230, 97.

179. Y. Li, E. Boone and M. A. El-Sayed, Langmuir, 2002, 18, 4921.

180. T. Teranishi and M. Miyake, Chem. Mater., 1998, 10, 594.

181. L. Balogh and D. A. Tomalia, J. Am. Chem. Soc., 1998, 120, 7355.

182. M. Q. Zhao, L. Sun and R. M. Crooks, J. Am. Chem. Soc., 1998, 120, 4877.

183. K. Esumi, T. Hosoya, A. Suzuki and K. Torigoe, Langmuir, 2000, 16, 2978.

184. Y. Li and M. A. El-Sayed, J. Phys. Chem. B, 2001, 105, 8938.

185. F. Hapiot, J. Lyskawa, H. Bricout, S. Tilloy and E. Monflier, Adv. Synth. Catal., 2004, 346, 83.

186. E. A. Katayev, Y. A. Ustynyuk and J. L. Sessler, Coord. Chem. Rev., 2006, 250, 3004.

187. L. Strimbu, J. Liu and A. E. Kaifer, Langmuir, 2003, 19, 483.

188. E. Garcia-Garrido, J. Francos, V. Cadierno, J. M. Basset, V. Polshettiwar, ChemSusChem, 2011, 4, 104.

189. V. Polshettiwar and R. S. Varma, Org. Biomol. Chem., 2009, 7, 37.

190. V. Polshettiwar, B. Baruwati and R. S. Varma, Green Chem., 2009, 11, 127.

191. Y. S. Chhonker, B. Veenu, S. R. Hasim, N. Kaushik, D. Kumar and P. Kumar, Eur. J. Chem., 2009, 6, 342;

192. R. Chebolu, D. N. Kommi, D. Kumar, N. Bollineni and A. K. Chakraborti, J. Org. Chem., 2012, 77, 10158;

193. R. Vinodkumar, S. D. Vaidya, B. V. S. Kumar, U. N. Bhise, S. B. Bhirud and U. C. Mashelkar, ARKIVOC, 2008(xiv), 37;

194. P. Bandyopadhyay, M. Sathe, S. Ponmariappan, A. Sharma, P. Sharma, A. K. Srivastava and M. P. Kaushik, Bioorg. Med. Chem. Lett., 2011, 21, 7306;

195. K. Bahrami, M. M. Khodaei and F. Naali, J. Org. Chem., 2008, 73, 6835;

196. Y. Kim, M. R. Kumar, N. Park, Y. Heo and S. Lee, J. Org. Chem., 2011, 76, 9577;

197. L. H. Du and Y. G. Wang, Synthesis, 2007, 5, 675–678; (h) M. Breza and V. Milata, ARKIVOC, 2005(ix), 80; (i) Z. G. Le, Z. C. Chen, Y. Hu and Q. G. Zheng, Synthesis, 2004, 2, 208.

198. R. S. Joshi, P. G. Mandhane, S. K. Dabhade and C. H. Gill, J. Chin. Chem. Soc., 2010, 57, 1227.

199. H. Yun, J. Yang, B. Wu, D. Robinson, K. Sprankle, P. P. Kung, K. Lowery, V. Mohan, S. Hofstadler, E. E. Swayze and R. Griffey, Bioorg. Med. Chem. Lett., 2004, 14, 695.

200. A. Grassi, J. Ippen, M. Bruno, G. Thomas and P. Bay, Eur. J. Pharmacol., 1991, 195, 251;

201. Y. Ozkay, Y. Tunali, H. Karaca and I. Isikdag, Eur. J. Med. Chem., 2010, 45, 3293.

202. M. Tonelli, M. Simone, B. Tasso, F. Novelli, V. Boido, F. Sparatore, G. Paglietti, S. Pricl, G. Giliberti, S. Blois, C. Ibba, G. Sanna, R. Loddo and P. La Colla, Bioorg. Med. Chem., 2010, 18, 2937.

203. Z. Kazimierczuk, J. A. Upcro, P. Upcro, A. G´orska, B. Starooeciak and A. Laudy, Acta Biochim. Pol., 2002, 49, 185.

204. Y. Tamura, N. Omori, N. Kouyama, Y. Nishiura, K. Hayashi, T. Watanabe, Y. Tanaka, T. Chiba, H. Yukioka, H. Sato and T. Okuno, Bioorg. Med. Chem. Lett., 2012, 22, 5498.

205. X. J. Wang, N. Y. Chu, Q. H. Wang, C. Liu, C. G. Jiang, X. Y. Wang, T. Ikejima and M. S. Cheng, Bioorg. Med. Chem. Lett., 2012, 22, 6297.

206. Hoebrecker, F., 1872. Ber. 5, 920-6.

207. C. T. Brain, S. A. Brunton, Tetrahedron Lett. 2002, 43, 1893 –1895;

208. C. T. Brain, J. T. Steer, J. Org. Chem. 2003, 68, 6814 –6816.

209. D. S. Surry, S. L. Buchwald, Angew. Chem. 2008, 120, 6438 –6461; Angew. Chem. Int. Ed. 2008, 47, 6338 –6361.

210. F. Monnier, M. Taillefer, Angew. Chem. 2009, 121, 7088 – 7105; Angew. Chem. Int. Ed. 2009, 48, 6954 –6971.

211. P. Saha, T. Ramana, N. Purkait, M. Ali, R. Paul, T. Punniyamurthy, J. Org. Chem. 2009, 74, 8719 –8725.

212. D. Yang, X. Zhu, W. Wei, N. Sun, L. Yuan, M. Jiang, J. Youac, H. Wang. RSC Adv., 2014, 4, 17832

213. S. Roy, B. Banerjee, N. Salam, A. Bhaumik, Sk. M. Islam Chem Cat Chem 2015, 7, 2689 – 2697

214. A. Teimouri, A. Najafi, Chermahini, H. Salavati, L. Ghorbanianc Journal of Molecular Catalysis A: Chemical 373 (2013) 38–45

215. I.J. Turchi, M.J.S. Dewar, Chem. Rev. 75 (1975) 389

216. V.S.C. Yeh, Tetrahedron 60 (2004) 11995

217. C.A. Zificsak, D.J. Hlasta, Tetrahedron 60 (2004) 8991.

218. A.D. Rodriguez, C. Ramirez, I.I. Rodriguez, E. Gonzalez, Org. Lett. 1 (1999) 527

219. J.P. Davidson, E.J. Corey, J. Am. Chem. Soc. 125 (2003) 13486.

220. M. Ueki, K. Ueno, S. Miyadoh, K. Abe, K. Shibata, M. Taniguchi, S. Oi, J. Antibiot. 46 (1993) 1089.

221. S. Sato, T. Kajiura, M. Noguchi, K. Takehana, T. Kobayashi, T. Tsuji, J. Antibiot. 54 (2001) 102.

222. M.J. Don, C.C. Shen, Y.L. Lin, W. Syu, Y.H. Ding Jr., C.M. Sun, J. Nat. Prod. 68 (2005) 1066.

223. D.C. Tully, H. Liu, P.B. Alper, A.K. Chatterjee, R. Epple, M.J. Roberts, J.A. Williams, K.T. Nguyen, D.H. Woodmansee, C. Tumanut, J. Li, G. Spraggon, J. Chang, T. Tuntland, J.L. Harris, D.S. Karanewsky, Bioorg. Med. Chem. Lett. 16 (2006) 1975.

224. X. Jiang, W. Tang, H. Dou, W. Zhang, C. Liu, J. Wang, J. Zheng, J. Inorg. Biochem. 104 (2010) 583.

225. S. Yoshida, S. Shiokawa, K. Kawano, T. Ito, H. Murakami, H. Suzuki, Y. Sato, J. Med. Chem. 48 (2005) 7075.

226. J.A. Grobler, G. Dornadula, M.R. Rice, A.L. Simcoe, D.J. Hazuda, M.D. Miller, J. Biol. Chem. 282 (2007) 8005.

227. L. Leventhal, M.R. Brandt, T.A. Cummons, M.J. Piesla, K.E. Rogers, H.A. Harris, Eur. J. Pharmacol. 553 (2006) 146.

228. J. Nishiu, M. Ito, Y. Ishida, M. Kakutani, T. Shibata, M. Matsushita, M. Shindo, Diabetes, Obes. Metab. 8 (2006) 508-516.

229. K. Rasmussen, M.A. Hsu, Y. Yang, Neuropsychopharmacology 32 (2007) 786.

230. P.D. Edwards, M.A. Zottola, M. Davis, J. Williams, P.A. Tuthill, J. Med. Chem. 38 (1995) 3972.

231. I.H. Leaver, B. Milligan, Dyes Pigm. 5 (1984) 109.

232. B.M. Krasovitskii, B.M. Bolotin, Organic Luminescent Materials, VCH, Weinheim, 1988.

233. M. Calle, Y.M. Lee, Macromolecules 44 (2011) 1156.

234. Y. Tian, C.Y. Chen, C.C. Yang, A.C. Young, S.H. Jang, W.C. Chen, A.K.Y. Jen, Chem. Mater. 20 (2008) 1977.

235. T.R. Chen, J. Organomet. Chem. 693 (2008) 3117.

236. R.S. Varma, D. Kumar, J. Heterocycl. Chem. 35 (1998) 1539.

237. J. Chang, K. Zhao, S. Pan, Tetrahedron Lett. 43 (2002) 951.

238. K.H. Park, K. Jun, S.R. Shin, S.W. Oh, Tetrahedron Lett. 37 (1996) 8869.

239. K. Nakagawa, H. Onoue, J. Sugita, Chem. Pharm. Bull. 12 (1964) 1135.

240. I.M. Baltork, A.R. Khosropour, S.F. Hojati, Catal. Commun. 8 (2007) 1865.

241. C. Praveen, K.H. Kumar, D. Muralidharan, P.T. Perumal, Tetrahedron 64 (2008) 2369.

242. D.S. Bose, M. Idrees, Synthesis 3 (2010) 398.

243. R.G. Srivastava, P.S. Venkataramani, Synth. Commun. 18 (1988) 1537.

244. F.F. Stephens, J.D. Bower, J. Chem. Soc. (1949) 2971.

245. K. Ravi Kumar, P.V.V. Satyanarayana, B. Srinivasa Reddy, Pharma. Chem. 4 (2012) 761.

246. V.S. Padalkar, V.D. Gupta, K.R. Phatangare, V.S. Patil, P.G. Umape, N. Sekar, Green Chem. Lett. Rev. 5 (2012) 139.

247. I.M. Baltork, M. Moghadam, S. Tangestaninejad, V. Mirkhani, M.A. Zolfigol, S.F. Hojati, J. Iran. Chem. Soc. 5 (2008) 65.

248. D. Kumar, S. Rudrawar, A.K. Chakraborti, Aust. J. Chem. 61 (2008) 881.

249. M.M. Guru, M.A. Ali, T. Punniyamurthy, Org. Lett. 13 (2011) 1194.

250. P. Saha, T. Ramana, N. Purkait, A. Ali, R. Paul, T. Punniyamurthy, J. Org. Chem. 74 (2009) 8719.

251. C.S. Cho, D.T. Kim, J.Q. Zhang, S.L. Ho, T.J. Kim, S.C. Shim, J. Heterocycl. Chem. 39 (2002) 421.

252. R.R. Nagawade, D.B. Shinde, Chin. Chem. Lett. 17 (2006) 453.

253. A.J. Blacker, M.M. Farah, S.P. Marsden, O. Saidi, J.M.J. Williams, Tetrahedron Lett. 50 (2009) 6106.

254. Y. Endo, J.E. Backvall, Chem.dEur. J. 18 (2012) 13609.

255. D. Yang, P. Liu, N. Zhang, W. Wei, M. Yue, J. You, H. Wang, ChemCatChem 6 (2014) 3434.

256. Y. Kawashita, N. Nakamichi, H. Kawabata, M. Hayashi, Org. Lett. 5 (2003) 3713.

257. R.G. Xing, Y.N. Li, Q. Liu, Q.Y. Meng, J. Li, X.X. Shen, Z. Liu, B. Zhou, X. Yao, Z.L. Liu, Eur. J. Org. Chem. (2010) 6627.

258. D. Suresh, A. Dhakshinamoorthy, K. Pitchumani, Tetrahedron Lett. 54 (2013) 6415.

259. S. Banerjee, J. Das, S. Santra, Tetrahedron Lett. 50 (2009) 124.

260. S.M. Inamdar, V.K. More, S.K. Mandal, Tetrahedron Lett. 54 (2013) 579.

261. S. Banerjee, S. Payra, A. Saha, G. Sereda, Tetrahedron Lett. 55 (2014) 5515.

262. R. Shelkar, S. Sarode, J. Nagarkar, Tetrahedron Lett. 54 (2013) 6986.

263. H. Naeimi, S. Rahmatinejad, Z.S. Nazifi, J. Taiwan Inst. Chem. Eng. 56 (2016) 1.

264. S.A. Sarode, J.M. Bhojane, J.M. Nagarkar, Tetrahedron Lett. 56 (2015) 206.

265. B. Maleki, M. Baghayeri, S.M. Vahdat, A. Mohammadzadeh, S. Akhoondi, RSC Adv. 5 (2015) 46545.

266. Novoselov KS, Geim AK, Morozov SV, Jiang D, Zhang Y, Dubonos SV, Grigorieva IV, Firsov AA. Electric field effect in atomically thin carbon films. Sci. 2004;306:666.

267. Du X, Skachko I, Barker A, Andrei EY. Approaching ballistic transport in suspended graphene. Nat Nanotechnol. 2008;3:491.

268. Lee C, Wei X, Kysar JW, Hone J. Measurement of the elastic properties and intrinsic strength of monolayer graphene. Sci. 2008;321:385.

269. Balandin AA, Ghosh S, Bao W, Calizo I, Teweldebrhan D, Miao F, Lau CN. Superior thermal conductivity of single-layer graphene. Nano Lett. 2008;8:902.

270. Jiang HJ. Chemical preparation of graphene-based nanomaterials and their applications in chemical and biological sensors. Small. 2011;7:2413.

271. Yang SB, Feng XL, Mullen K. Sandwich-like, graphene-based titania nanosheets with high surface area for fast lithium storage. Adv Mater. 2011;23:3575.

272. Xiang QJ, Yu JG, Jaroniec M. Synergetic effect of MoS_2 and graphene as cocatalysts for enhanced photocatalytic H_2 production activity of TiO_2 nanoparticles. J Am Chem Soc. 2012;134:6575.

273. Kim KS, Zhao Y, Jang H, Lee SY, Kim JM, Kim KS, Ahn J-H, Kim P, Choi J-Y, Hong BH. Large-scale pattern growth of graphene films for stretchable transparent electrodes. Nature. 2009;457:706.

274. Pei SF, Cheng HM. The reduction of graphene oxide. Carbon. 2012;50:3210.

275. Geng J, Kong BS, Yang SB, Jung HT. Preparation of graphene relying on porphyrin exfoliation of graphite. Chem Commun. 2010;46:5091.

276. Kosynkin DV, Higginbotham AL, Sinitskii A, Lomeda JR, Dimiev A, Price1 BK, Tour JM. Longitudinal unzipping of carbon nanotubes to form graphene nanoribbons. Nat. 2009;458:872.

277. Choucair M, Thordarson P, Stride JA. Gram-scale production of graphene based on solvothermal synthesis and sonication. Nat Nanotechnol. 2009;4:30.

278. Reina A, Jia XT, Ho J, Nezich D, Son H, Bulovic V, Dresselhaus MS, Kong J. Large area, few-layer graphene films on arbitrary substrates by chemical vapor deposition. Nano Lett. 2009;9:30.

279. Li XS, Cai WW, An JB, Kim S, Nah J, Yang DX, Piner R, Velamakanni A, Jung I, Tutuc E, Banerjee SK, Colombo L, Ruoff RS. Large-area synthesis of high-quality and uniform graphene films on copper foils. Sci. 2009;324:1312.

280. Bae S, Kim H, Lee Y, Xu XF, Park JS, Zheng Y, Balakrishnan J, Lei T, Kim HR, Song YI, Kim YJ, Kim KS, Ozyilmaz B, Ahn JH, Hong BH, Iijima S. Roll-to-roll production of 30-inch graphene films for transparent electrodes. Nat Nanotechnol. 2010;5:574.

281. Bell NJ, Ng YH, Du AJ, Coster H, Smith SC, Amal R. Understanding the enhancement in photoelectrochemical properties of photocatalytically prepared TiO2-reduced graphene oxide composite. J Phys Chem C. 2011;115:6004.

282. Huang XD, Zhou XF, Zhou L, Qian K, Wang YH, Liu ZP, Yu CZ. A facile one-step solvothermal synthesis of SnO2/graphene nanocomposite and its application as an anode material for lithium-Ion batteries. Chem Phys Chem. 2011;12:278.

283. Koo HY, Lee HJ, Go HA, Lee YB, Bae TS, Kim JK, Choi WS. Graphene-based multifunctional iron oxide nanosheets with tunable properties. Chem Eur J. 2011;17:1214.

284. Schniepp HC, Li JL, McAllister MJ, Sai H, Herrera-Alonso M, Adamson DH, Prud'homme RK, Car R, Saville DA, Aksay IA. Functionalized single graphene sheets derived from splitting graphite oxide. J Phys Chem B. 2006;110:8535.

285. Gao XF, Jang J, Nagase S. Hydrazine and thermal reduction of graphene oxide: Reaction mechanisms, product structures, and reaction design. J

Phys Chem C. 2010;114:832.

286. Ramesha GK, Sampath S. Electrochemical reduction of oriented graphene oxide films: An in situ raman spectroelectrochemical study. J Phys Chem C. 2009;113:7985.

287. Abdelsayed V, Moussa S, Hassan HM, Aluri HS, Collinson MM, El-Shall MS. Photothermal deoxygenation of graphite oxide with laser excitation in solution and graphene-aided increase in water temperature. J Phys Chem Lett. 2010;1:2804.

288. Ng YH, Lightcap IV, Goodwin K, Matsumura M, Kamat PV. To what extent do graphene scaffolds improve the photovoltaic and photocatalytic response of TiO2 nanostructured films? J Phys Chem Lett. 2010;1:2222.

289. Vinodgopal K, Neppolian B, Lightcap IV, Grieser F, Ashokkumar M, Kamat PV. Sonolytic design of graphene–Au nanocomposites. Simultaneous and sequential reduction of graphene oxide and Au (III). J Phys Chem Lett. 2010;1:1987.

290. Jasuja K, Linn J, Melton S, Berry V. Microwave-reduced uncapped metal nanoparticles on graphene: Tuning catalytic, electrical, and raman properties. J Phys Chem Lett. 2010;1:1853.

291. Paek S-M, Yoo E, Honma I. Enhanced cyclic performance and lithium storage capacity of SnO_2/graphene nanoporous electrodes with three-dimensionally delaminated flexible structure. Nano Lett. 2009;9:72.

292. Williams G, Seger B, Kamat PV. TiO2-graphene nanocomposites. UV-assisted photocatalytic reduction of graphene oxide. ACS Nano. 2008;2:1487.

293. Sun SR, Gao L, Liu YQ. Enhanced dye-sensitized solar cell using graphene-TiO2 photoanode prepared by heterogeneous coagulation. Appl Phys Lett. 2010;96:083113.

294. Akhavan O, Ghaderi E. Photocatalytic reduction of graphene oxide nanosheets on TiO2 thin film for photoinactivation of bacteria in solar light irradiation. J Phys Chem C. 2009;113:20214.

295. Zhang XY, Li HP, Cui XL, Lin YH. Graphene/TiO2 nanocomposites: synthesis, characterization and application in hydrogen evolution from water photocatalytic splitting. J Mater Chem. 2010;20:2801.

296. Du J, Lai XY, Yang NL, Zhai J, Kisailus D, Su FB, Wang D, Jiang L. Hierarchically ordered macro-mesoporous TiO2-graphene composite films: Improved mass transfer, reduced charge recombination, and their enhanced photocatalytic activities. ACS Nano. 2011;5:590.

297. Yang SB, Feng XL, Wang L, Tang K, Maier J, Mullen K. Graphene-based nanosheets with a sandwich structure. Angew Chem Int Ed. 2010;49:4795.

298. Xiang QJ, Yu JG, Jaroniec M. Enhanced photocatalytic H2-production activity of graphenemodified titania nanosheets. Nanoscale. 2011;3:3670.

299. Jiang BJ, Tian CG, Pan QJ, Jiang Z, Wang JQ, Yan WS, Fu HG. Enhanced photocatalytic activity and electron transfer mechanisms of graphene/ TiO2 with exposed {001} facets. J Phys Chem C. 2011;115:23718.

300. He ZM, Guai GH, Liu J, Guo CX, Loo JSC, Li Ming C, Tan TTY. Nanostructure control of graphene-composited TiO2 by a one-step solvothermal approach for high performance dyesensitized solar cells. Nanoscale. 2011;3:4613.

301. Wang JZ, Zhong C, Wexler D, Idris NH, Wang ZX, Chen LQ, Liu HK. Graphene-encapsulated Fe3O4 nanoparticles with 3D laminated structure as superior anode in lithium ion batteries. Chem Eur J. 2011;17:661.

302. Zhu JX, Sharma YK, Zeng ZY, Zhang XJ, Srinivasan M, Mhaisalkar S, Zhang H, Hng HH, Yan QY. Cobalt oxide nanowall arrays on reduced graphene oxide sheets with controlled phase, grain size, and porosity for li-ion battery electrodes. J Phys Chem C. 2011;115:8400.

303. Wang DH, Kou R, Choi DW, Yang ZG, Nie ZM, Li J, Saraf LV, Hu DH, Zhang JG, Graff GL, Liu J, Pope MA, Aksay IA. Ternary self-assembly of ordered metal oxide-graphene nanocomposites for electrochemical energy storage. ACS Nano. 2010;4:1587.

304. Hao OJ, Kim H, Chiang PC. Decolorization of wastewater. Crit Rev Environ Sci Technol 2000;30:449– 502.

305. Tunay O, Kabdasli I, Eremektar G, Orhon D. Color removal from textile wastewaters. Water Sci Technol 1996;34:9–16.

306. Zhang H, Lv XJ, Li YM, Wang Y, Li JH. P25-graphene composite as a high performance photocatalyst. ACS Nano. 2010;4:380.

307. Chen C, Cai WM, Long MC, Zhou BX, Wu YH, Wu DY, Feng YJ. Synthesis of visible-light responsive graphene oxide/TiO2 composites with p/n heterojunction. ACS Nano. 2010;4:6425.

308. Lee JS, You KH, Park CB. Highly photoactive, low bandgap TiO2 nanoparticles wrapped by graphene. Adv Mater. 2012;24:1084.